No

Early maps of London's

Need to

Underground Railways

Ask!

David Leboff

and

Tim Demuth

Capital Transport

First published 1999

ISBN 185414 215 1

Published by Capital Transport Publishing,
38 Long Elmes, Harrow Weald, Middlesex

Designed by Tim Demuth

Printed by CS Graphics, Singapore

© Capital Transport 1999

Acknowledgements

We would like to thank those who have assisted us during the
production of this book, and in particular Mike Horne, Sheila
Taylor, Peter Bancroft, Alan Blake, Doug Rose, Michael
Hellings, David Cutter and many others, for their advice and
criticism. We are also grateful to the London Transport
Museum, Stan and Val Friedman, Dave Jones, the staff at the
Hertfordshire County Archives & Local Studies Department,
the Public Record Office, British Library and Bodleian Library.
Thanks are also due to numerous other collectors for
permission to reproduce certain maps, posters and
photographs in their possession, and finally, to David's wife
Sara for her encouragement and Jim Whiting for his faith in
our endeavours.

TITLE PAGE
Maps of the Underground are
serious affairs, not noted for the
humour and frivolity often
appearing on posters and press
advertising. We don't know the exact
brief to the artist John Hassal. What
is known is that the poster (on which
the front cover and title of this book
are based) coincided with the
appearance of one of the first
comprehensive maps of the
Underground system in 1908, so it
seems likely that it was specifically
produced to advertise the fact.
Hassal has taken his brief a stage
further, by implying that the map is
very simple to understand,
something that may not have been
appreciated immediately by
passengers seeing it for the first
time. The choice of subject matter
would have been the artist's, such
was his original thinking.

ABBREVIATIONS OF RAILWAY, TRAM AND BUS COMPANIES

BR	British Railways	**LNER**	London & North Eastern Railway
BSWR	Baker Street & Waterloo Railway	**LPTB**	London Passenger Transport Board
CCEHR	Charing Cross, Euston & Hampstead Railway	**LSWR**	London & South Western Railway
CLR	Central London Railway	**LTSR**	London Tilbury & Southend Railway
CSLR	City & South London Railway	**LUT**	London United Tramways
ELR	East London Railway	**MSJWR**	Metropolitan & St John's Wood Railway
GER	Great Eastern Railway	**MDR**	Metropolitan District Railway
GNPBR	Great Northern, Piccadilly & Brompton Railway		
GWR	Great Western Railway	**MET**	Metropolitan Electric Tramways
LBSC	London Brighton & South Coast Railway	**Met**	Metropolitan Railway
		MSLR	Manchester Sheffield & Lincolnshire Railway
LCC	London County Council (Tramways)	**SER**	South Eastern Railway
LCDR	London Chatham & Dover Railway	**UERL**	Underground Electric Railways Company of London, Ltd
LER	London Electric Railway		
LGOC	London General Omnibus Company Ltd	**WCR**	Waterloo & City Railway
LMS	London Midland & Scottish Railway		

Contents

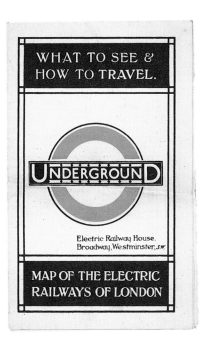

Foreword

The London Underground diagrammatic map is so well known throughout the world that it needs little description, except to say that it has become an icon of the capital since it first appeared in 1933. Its birth is dealt with in this book's companion volume: *Mr Beck's Underground Map*. The fact that diagrammatic maps of differing styles reflecting the expanding system have decorated Underground stations and have been carried in pockets and handbags for over 60 years can lead to an assumption that the Underground network has always been portrayed in this style. However, the very reason for using a diagrammatic form is because of the shortcomings of communicating a rapidly growing and increasingly intricate urban rail network using traditional cartographic methods. The geographic presentation of London's underground railways has used styles ranging from a simple superimposition of the lines onto existing street plans, to the system drawn in its own right, very often utilising attractive and artistic styles. A bold simple approach has always been the prime aim in this early and long lived form of publicity design. This book aims to illustrate some of the wide range of various styles of map that were used to describe the Underground system, before the diagrammatic approach simplified the interpretation of a complicated and expanding system.

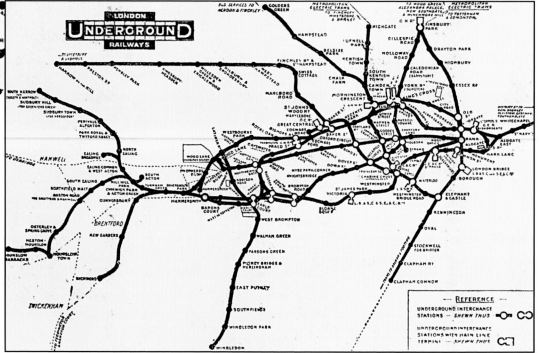

This map was produced in 1908 by the Underground Group as a standard artwork for inclusion in commercial publications.

The treatment of stations (as solid circles) and interchange stations (as open circles) can be clearly seen – the interchange treatment anticipating that in use on today's diagrammatic maps.

The Underground Group's own lines have been supplemented by those that they considered to be complementary to their own. Hence the inclusion of the London & South Western Railway's line, on which the District Railway ran over the Turnham Green to Barons Court section and the Great Western's Richmond trains ran over the rest, via Hammersmith Grove Road.

Chapter 1 The making of maps

BRADSHAW'S RAILWAY MAP 1890
Inset into a map of Great Britain, this map of London's railways was engraved in the same style since first appearing in the 1840s.

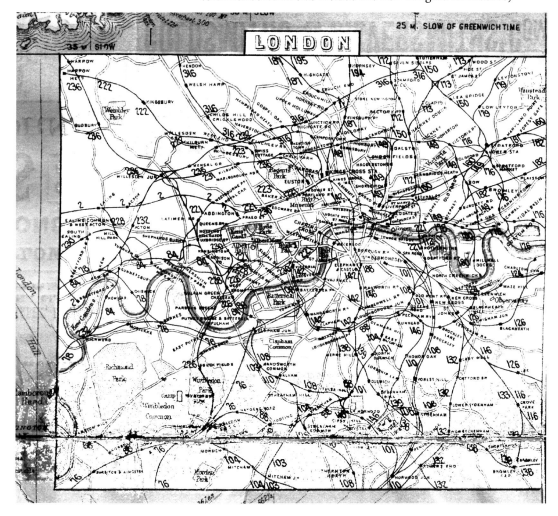

At the time that the first underground railway was opened in 1863, the mapping of Britain's railways was already well established. George Bradshaw, better known for his famous all-embracing rail timetables, was originally trained as a map engraver and produced some of the first maps showing the established canals as well as the new fangled rail routes, requiring frequent new editions as they rapidly invaded the country in the 1830s and '40s. Whilst additions could usually be made to an existing engraving, most other changes of any size would need a completely new one from the base drawing.

For the production of thousands of printed copies only two methods were feasible, both making use of the raised surface of the original to separate the transfer of ink to paper. Printing from the raised surface of metal or wood was the usual way by which books and posters were produced. Any illustrations were cut with chisel by hand, usually onto wood, which meant that any detail had to remain quite coarse. This method is called letterpress. The other method utilised printing from the ink caught between the indentations in the raised surface. This was engraving, where the gaps could be as delicate as a thin scratch. A metal sheet was coated with wax and the image was then scribed through to the metal. When complete, the sheet was immersed in acid which bit into the metal exposed by the scribing, leaving fine scribed indentations. For printing, ink was rolled over the surface of the plate which was then scraped clean to leave the ink only in the indentations. When the plate, with paper on the surface, was squeezed in the press the ink would transfer from the indentations of the plate to the paper. As with letterpress printing, the inked surface had to be produced in mirror form so that it would be seen on the printed paper the correct way round. Engravers could get over this limitation by drawing their originals the correct way round onto tracing paper, which was then ironed face down onto the wax surface of the plate. When the paper was peeled away the drawing was left on the surface in mirror form, ready to be scribed. Engraving was ideally suited to the production of maps, which were mainly linear and did not need to include large areas of dark shading. When this was required, the engraved scratches were drawn very close to each other. For more solid colours a letterpress block could be made for overprinting, or, alternatively, the image drawn back to front onto a litho stone also for overprinting.

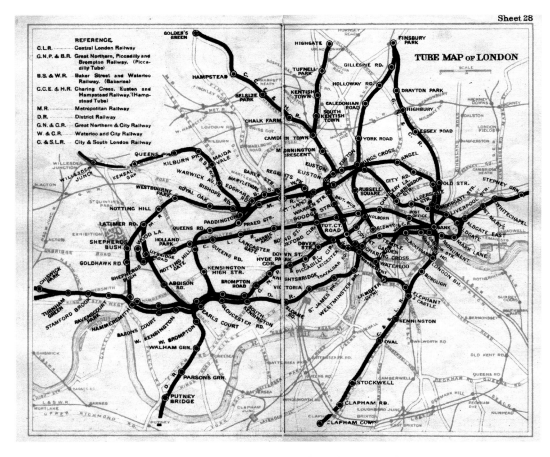

BACONS GUIDE 1918
Printed in their street plan of London guidebook this map is very much the work of the publisher's art department. While taking most of its design elements from existing maps produced for and by the Underground Group, some would have been new to this map.

The arrival of lithography

The presentation of maps during the nineteenth century was dictated by the limitations of the engraving process. These limitations were removed towards the end of that century when lithography became commercially feasible.

Lithography exploited the fact that oil and water do not mix. By drawing an image onto a stone with a wax based crayon or brush and then damping the entire stone with water, the oil-based printing ink would only adhere to the waxy image. As with other forms of printing until the start of the twentieth century, the image had to be applied back to front so that it would appear the right way round when printed onto paper. Offset lithographic printing machines came into general use from about 1908, allowing, by means of printing onto the paper through an intermediate roller, the image to be drawn the correct way round. Whilst engraved maps held the advantage over lithographic maps in the fineness of line that could be applied, it was found that by using special wax based

inks to print from the engraving to the paper, the paper could then be applied to the litho stone leaving its ink on the stone. This method was also used to transfer the image of letterpress printing types onto litho stones. By the end of the 1930s lightweight zinc plates had generally replaced litho stones.

With the advent of photographically based copper plates to produce halftones by letterpress, the same basic method was used to transfer an image from a photographic negative or positive to a litho stone. Photo litho also allowed the original to be drawn onto a separate surface (called artwork) and photographed, instead of drawing directly onto the plate. Artwork was usually a smooth quality paper that would accept pen strokes without them spreading. Since photography had been brought into the process, the artwork could be drawn any size (usually larger than the printed size) and photographically adjusted to the final size. This meant that small items could be drawn much larger, giving the fineness associated with engraving when reduced in size. Photography also meant that any lettering could be set in type, printed as a patch, cut out and pasted onto the artwork. These advances shifted the job of engraver or litho artist to the artworker. As map production became more publicity orientated, the cartographer enhanced his specialist skills as a researcher while the designer interpreted the cartographer's work. The designer therefore became paramount in initiating the planned look of a map, from the cartographer's 'working drawings' to the overseeing of artworkers and (perhaps) calligraphers who would produce the mechanically correct original for photographing onto the litho plate. It is, therefore, the constraints as well as the possibilities of printing processes that have had as great an influence on the development of maps as a form of communicative publicity as have the ideas of the craftsmen designing those maps.

The purpose of a map is to show an area as accurately as possible to its actual topography. However, maps and plans of urban areas have to be distorted if they are drawn to a small scale, to allow detailed information such as place and road names to be accommodated. The Ordnance Survey had, on their maps since the mid-nineteenth century, applied the names of roads down the middles of roads. When the Metropolitan Railway was built beneath London's streets, the line of railway overprinted on a street plan would have rendered the street names unreadable. This was solved to some extent by drawing the route of the rail line beside the roads instead of over them.

The publicity value of showing the line was now becoming more apparent. Because lines were usually overprinted onto existing maps there was no practical reason why a colour not already in use should not be added, for instance, bright red overprinted onto a map printed in black.

By the time the Metropolitan and Metropolitan District railways arrived on the scene, railway maps were well established. In 1827 George Bradshaw had started an engraving business in Manchester specialising in maps showing navigable rivers and canals and adding passenger carrying railways as they opened. When William Blacklock and a letterpress printer named Robert Kay joined the Bradshaw business in the 1830s, Bradshaw's Railway Guide was born. Issued monthly, it contained timetables and maps of all railway routes operating in Great Britain.

The Metropolitan and District railways appear to have initially made use of Bradshaw's Guide to promote their services. Later both, and in particular the District, were to produce their own publicity material; its development is outlined in Chapter 2.

Cartographic artists

Very few names of individuals are mentioned on maps because they were regarded as 'in house' technicians, even if we now regard some of the more decorative examples illustrated in later chapters as works of art in their own right. Some indication can be gained as to the originator by studying the printer's name, usually in tiny type hidden in a bottom corner. As long as printers employed technicians, either as engravers or litho artists, a consecutive and developing service would be provided to the client. Customers would turn to a printer as much for the technical service and research done as for the price and delivery. A printer may have won a job because of the ideas being provided as much as for the printing expertise. As maps became more publicity orientated a printer may have considered it worth going outside of the premises to employ the freelance skills of an acknowledged expert.

Some printers' names appear consistently as suppliers of a developing source of art as well as good printing. There are the established cartographic printers who also doubled up as publishers, such as Bradshaw, Waterlow and McCorquodale – all of whom also generated a vast span of railway related printing work. Firms specialising entirely in cartography and its production were (and some still are) Edward Stanford, Geographia, George Philip & Son, R J Cook & Hammond and C F Kell & Son. Some grew to have a long association with the Underground Group and its successors. On the general printing side was the Dangerfield Printing Company, established in the 1850s as printers of illuminated gift books. Dangerfields took out patents for the advancement of lithographic printing, and built up an enviable reputation for their litho art and printing until World War II. Another was Johnson Riddle & Co, who continued its association with London Transport for nearly three quarters of a century until the late 1970s.

It is because of the anonymous expertise within these printing concerns that few map artists' names have come to the fore. One freelance artist who made enough impression on Underground maps to have his signature included was MacDonald Gill. He specialised in intricate illustrations and calligraphy and is equally remembered for his illustrative maps and his ecclesiastical work, particularly in the form of stained glass windows. Then there was Fred Stingemore, described as a draughtsman within the Underground's Commercial Manager's Office, who would put his hand to almost anything, including drawings in the Underground Group's own staff magazine. We will return to these artists in Chapter 5.

UNDERGROUND MAP OF LONDON 1919
Appearing in the *Railway Year Book*, this was a piece of official Underground artwork, which would have been produced by one of their printers. A line block was made from the artwork, which was then incorporated into the text of the book which was printed letterpress.

Chapter 2 London's metropolitan railways

London's first Underground line was opened by the Metropolitan Railway on 10 January 1863, its construction arising mainly from a need of the main lines from the provinces for a link with the City and to provide a faster means of transit than by traffic choked roads for local journeys.

The original scheme to receive Royal Assent would have consisted of an eight-track sub-surface rail line from Paddington to a grand terminus at the southern end of Farringdon Street, on land that would have been cleared for rebuilding. Junctions were planned with the London & North Western Railway at Euston, and the Midland and the Great Northern railways at King's Cross. The money needed for this enterprise failed to materialise, so a less ambitious but similar scheme was drawn up with the financial backing of the City Corporation. This envisaged a terminus beside a new street linking Holborn Hill to Clerkenwell Green on land released by the move of the Smithfield Cattle Market to Copenhagen Fields. This land would also be used for goods yards to hold wagons emanating from the main line railways as part of the price of their financial support.

Stations were sited at Paddington Bishop's Road, Edgware Road, Baker Street, Portland Road (renamed Great Portland Street in 1917), Gower Street (renamed Euston Square in 1909), King's Cross (which, until it was closed in 1941, was to the east of the present King's Cross St Pancras) and Farringdon Street (renamed Farringdon & High Holborn in 1922 and reduced to just Farringdon in 1936). The original Farringdon Street station had a short life since it was built on a trajectory that would have taken the line towards Blackfriars (the Thameslink alignment later extended to link with the London Chatham & Dover Railway), but before the line was opened, powers were obtained to extend to Aldersgate Street (renamed Aldersgate & Barbican in 1923 and Barbican in 1968) and Moorgate Street (renamed Moorgate in 1924) at Finsbury Circus, the line opening in December 1865. The Metropolitan Railway was an immediate success, attracting 40,000 passengers on its first day and an average of nearly 30,000 passengers per day during its first six months.

A separate scheme was promoted by the Metropolitan District Railway – the construction of an inner circle line within central London, using the completed Metropolitan Railway as its northern portion. The Metropolitan, for its part, was authorised to extend the western end of its line from a point between Edgware Road and Bishop's Road to a new station, just south of Paddington GWR terminus, to be called Paddington (Praed Street); then to Bayswater, Kensington (High Street), Brompton (Gloucester Road) and South Kensington. In the east the line would be extended from Moorgate to Bishopsgate (renamed Liverpool Street in 1909), Aldgate and Tower of London. The District Railway would build from South Kensington and continue eastwards through Sloane Square, Victoria, St James's Park and Westminster Bridge. The Circle Line, as we know it today, was completed in 1884.

Since 1872 the Chairman of the Metropolitan had been Sir Edward Watkin. He was also Chairman of the Manchester Sheffield & Lincolnshire and the South Eastern railways.

METROPOLITAN RAILWAY
Some of the original stations were very spacious between the platforms in order to accommodate the broad (7ft 0¼in) as well as standard (4ft 8½in) gauge of the tracks. This was to allow Great Western Railway broad gauge trains, which worked the first service, to run through to the City from west London. This is King's Cross, which was built to the east of the present station. An impression of this style of architecture can still be gained at Paddington and Notting Hill Gate, both on the Circle Line, although neither featured broad gauge track and are therefore less spacious.

METROPOLITAN RAILWAY C.1867

13½ by 13¼ inches (34.5×34 cm)

This engraved map of around 1867 shows the original Metropolitan Railway opened on 10 January 1863 as a bold overprint as well as lines to Kensington (the present Kensington Olympia) opened in July 1864 and to Hammersmith and Moorgate opened in April and December the following year respectively.

Projected lines are shown as dotted – notably that of the Metropolitan & St John's Wood Railway which would open as far as Swiss Cottage in 1868. (The MSJWR was extended to Willesden, and not Hampstead as originally planned, in 1879 and incorporated into the more ambitious, and successful, Metropolitan Railway three years later.) Lines of other railways are in thinner red. The base black street plan was probably already held as an existing engraving by the printer, Kell Bros, since it depicts the whole of London as it existed in 1867 – far beyond the Metropolitan Railway's sphere of operations. The title was possibly a separate printing onto a standard engraving.

The advantage of overprinting the railways in red was that the base map could be used over and over again for separate editions, while the red overprint reflected London's growing rail system. The intention of overprinting in red rather than black would have avoided a problem where the railways did not fit onto the base street plan. This is a good example of how a practical solution to a printing limitation would have spawned the view that a separate colour could be used as an effective way to emphasise the railways. A later development was to print some railways in red and other less important (or directly competing) lines in a less prominent colour such as blue.

Metropolitan Railway and Connections c.1874 (right)
11½ by 8½ inches (29×21.5 cm)

This small folded map of the Metropolitan Railway was probably to be found in contemporary guidebooks of London.

It depicts the full extent of the railway around 1874, with the proposed extension to Bishopsgate (Liverpool Street) still under construction but no mention of the Metropolitan District Railway's westward extension from Earl's Court to Hammersmith, which opened in September of that year. An unusual feature is the lack of background detail, which contrasts sharply with the street plans used as the basis for most railway maps of the period.

The Metropolitan promoted horse-bus feeder services to several of its stations. Two of these are indicated on this map – the Portland Road [now Great Portland Street] to Piccadilly Circus route (which commenced as far as Oxford Circus in 1866, extended to Piccadilly Circus in February 1874 and ceased in December 1894) and the one from Gower Street [now Euston Square] to Camden Town (which operated between February 1874 and May 1880).

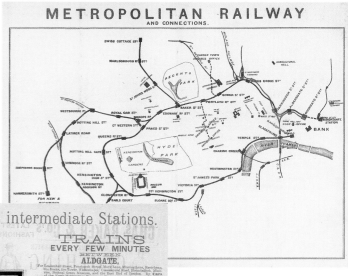

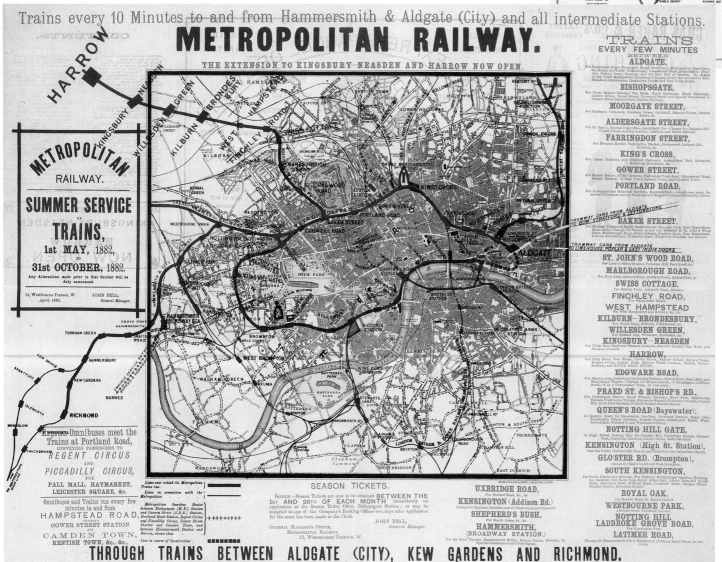

Metropolitan Railway c.1882
19½ by 15 inches (50×38 cm)

Few maps were issued by the Metropolitan Railway in its early years, certainly compared to the various series produced for the District Railway from 1874 onwards. However, versions were included in Met timetables, as this example, printed by Waterlows and contained within the May 1882 edition, illustrates.

The central section of the map, with its detailed street plan, is similar in style to that shown on page 9, but in this instance additional information about the station and train services is provided within the border. The map itself probably predates the timetable by two years, for the subtitle refers to the opening of the extension from Willesden Green to Harrow, which occurred in August 1880. However, the District Railway extension to Putney Bridge and Fulham, which opened six months earlier, is not shown.

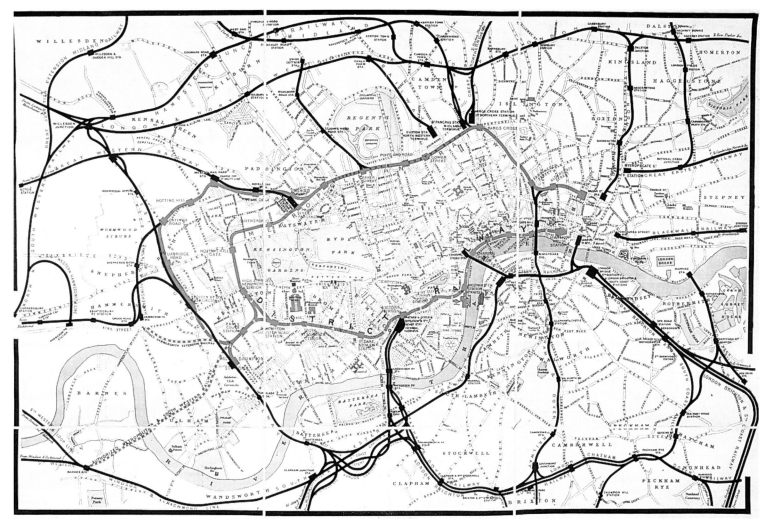

THE "DISTRICT" RAILWAY MAP OF LONDON 1874

39¼ by 24¾ inches
(100×63.5 cm)

This is perhaps the first map to be produced on behalf of any of the railways that were to form London's Underground. Published in 1874 by the still existing and well known cartographic publishers, Edward Stanford, it was printed by Waterlow & Sons who had already built up their business in the provision of the vast volume of printed material required in the running of any railway, from internal forms and waybills to items seen by the public such as posters and timetables.

The immense size of this map meant that it would have been of little use for those actually travelling, but may have been a general map of London adapted to distinguish the District Railway.

The street plan style is very much that used by Stanfords for their maps issued subsequently and well into the twentieth century. The rendering of the rail lines is very (and perhaps unnecessarily) accurate, as can be seen by the twisting of the Midland line north of King's Cross and equally the lines south of Victoria.

Of interest is the kink of the London Brighton & South Coast Railway which causes it to break into the right hand border, in order to maintain Westminster and the City in the centre of the map.

In 1874 the Inner Circle line of the Metropolitan and District railways

was still waiting to be completed between Mansion House and Moorgate Street. At the time of this map's publication, the Metropolitan District Railway had been open for only five years.

The first section, between West Brompton and the Metropolitan Railway's station at Brompton (Gloucester Road) was opened in April 1869, to be extended to Blackfriars via Westminster in May 1870 and on to Mansion House in July 1871. On this date the link between Earl's Court and High Street Kensington was also opened.

Extensions yet to be opened are those to Hammersmith (which

would compete with the jointly owned Metropolitan and Great Western Hammersmith & City line) and the planned Metropolitan & South Western Railway route from Earl's Court to Barnes, which like many other proposed schemes, was to flounder before building even started.

The front and back covers (*right*) are very definitely in the traditional letterpress style to be found on advertisements and title pages. While the typesetting is that of a competent journeyman, the layouts doing nothing to reflect the style of cartography to be found inside.

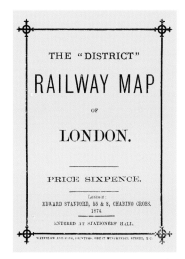

THE "DISTRICT"

RAILWAY MAP

OF

LONDON.

PRICE SIXPENCE.

LONDON:
EDWARD STANFORD, 55 & 8, CHARING CROSS.
1874.

ENTERED AT STATIONERS' HALL.

WATERLOW AND SONS, PRINTERS, GREAT WINCHESTER STREET, E.C.

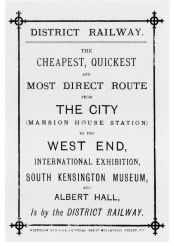

DISTRICT RAILWAY.

THE

CHEAPEST, QUICKEST

AND

MOST DIRECT ROUTE

FROM

THE CITY

(MANSION HOUSE STATION)

TO THE

WEST END,

INTERNATIONAL EXHIBITION,

SOUTH KENSINGTON MUSEUM,

AND

ALBERT HALL,

Is by the DISTRICT RAILWAY.

WATERLOW AND SONS, PRINTERS, GREAT WINCHESTER STREET, E.C.

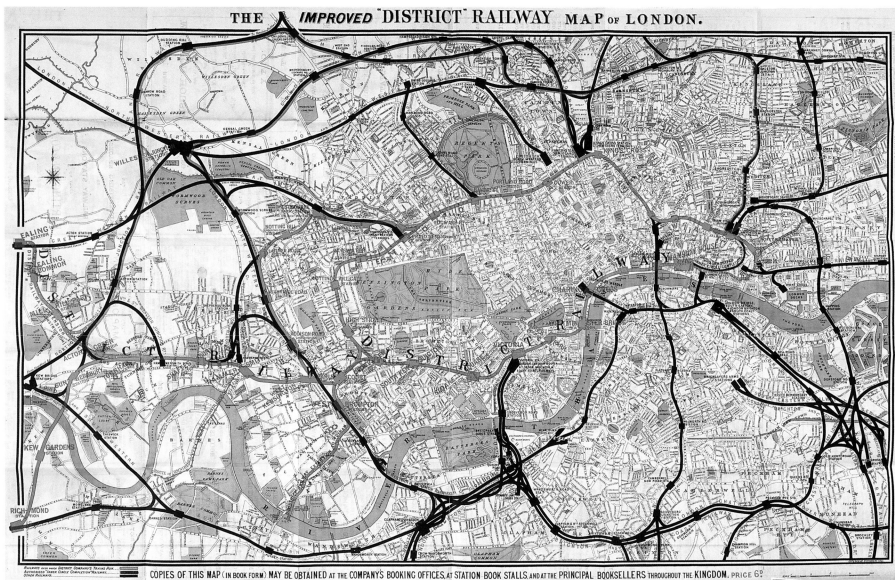

Railways over which District Company's Trains Run.
Authorised "Inner Circle Completion" Railway.
Other Railways.

COPIES OF THIS MAP (IN BOOK FORM) MAY BE OBTAINED AT THE COMPANY'S BOOKING OFFICES, AT STATION BOOK STALLS, AND AT THE PRINCIPAL BOOKSELLERS THROUGHOUT THE KINGDOM. PRICE 6ᴰ.

THE IMPROVED "DISTRICT RAILWAY" MAP OF LONDON 1879

41¾ by 26 inches (106×66 cm)

Waterlows used the experience gained by their production of the 1874 map in this version produced five years later.

Lines over which District Railway trains ran make use of red, while the authorised section of the as yet incomplete Inner Circle is in blue, all other lines being in black. Also

shown are the District Railway's extensions under construction to Fulham and from Turnham Green to Acton and Ealing.

Another difference from the earlier map is the repositioning of Earl's Court station. This is no mistake, since the original timber built station, when opened in October 1874, was sited to the east of Earl's Court Road, but was severely damaged by fire in December 1875.

A new brick street building, together with John Wolfe-Barry's magnificent train shed, was opened opposite the site of the original building in 1878.

The cover marks a creative departure from the plain style employed for previous map covers. The illustrations of prominent London landmarks and the steam locomotive interworked with the title make for an attractive and eye-catching piece of graphic design.

12

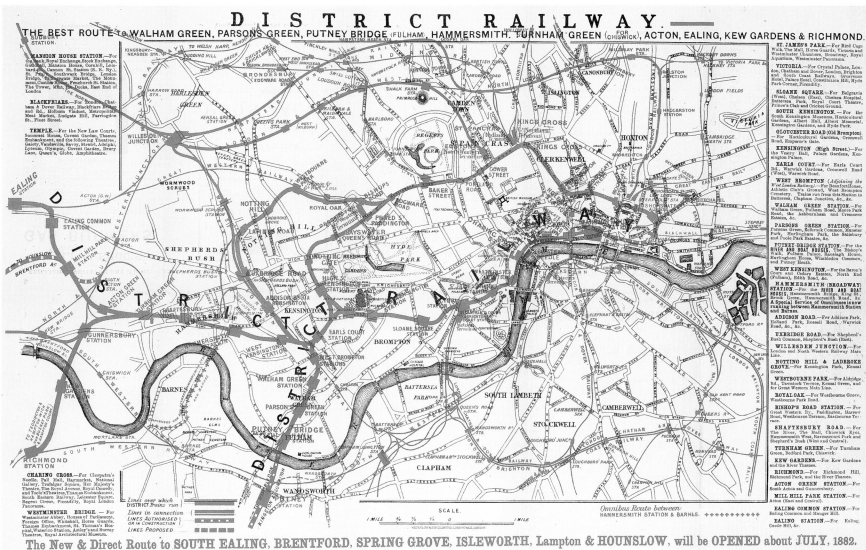

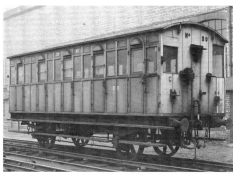

District Railway 1881

18 by 11½ inches (46×29 cm)

This map displays the continuous development into cartographic clarity, combined with the incorporation of useful letterpress information around the map.

Waterlows were also agents for the production of the advertisements that would have appeared on the reverse of this map, the revenue from them going a long way to offset the production and distribution costs of such a map. Although not given a particular name, this production formed a predecessor to what became known as the "Miniature Map" series that employed less detailed maps and folded to a smaller size, but more convenient for travellers' pockets.

(*right*) Locomotive and typical coach of the type running round the Inner Circle Line when it opened in 1884.

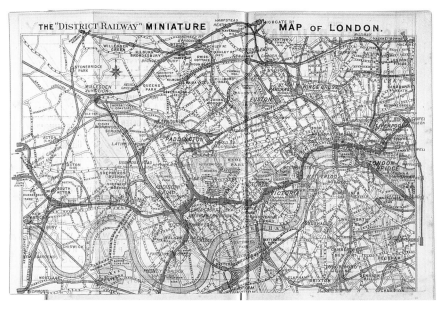

THE "DISTRICT RAILWAY" MINIATURE MAP OF LONDON.

THE 'DISTRICT RAILWAY' COUNTRY DIAGRAM 1883
(*left*)
11 *by* 17½ *inches* (28×45 cm)

From 1 March 1883, the Metropolitan District Railway gained running powers over the Great Western Railway's tracks between Ealing Common and Windsor. This map – the first of an irregular series – was issued as a promotion by the District Railway a few months after commencing its service to Windsor. In this respect, it was unsuccessful, for the service ceased in September 1885. The map is interesting in that it shows the almost complete Inner Circle, and projected extensions to Hounslow Barracks (opened July 1884), Surbiton (abandoned June 1886) and Wimbledon (opened, over a line built by the LSWR, June 1889). Also shown is the proposed extension of the Metropolitan Railway north of Harrow.

THE 'DISTRICT RAILWAY' MINIATURE MAP OF LONDON c.1886 (*above*)
10½ *by* 6¾ *inches* (26.5×17.5 cm)

This later version of the Miniature Map series was bound into a volume of Routledge's Guide to London. The red station names fail to stand out against the intensive black street layout. The American Exhibition at Earl's Court is worth noting.

THE 'DISTRICT RAILWAY' MAP OF LONDON c.1892
(*opposite*)
42¼ *by* 26¼ *inches* (107×67 cm)

The District Railway map was developed and improved throughout the 1880s and '90s, new editions often necessitated by the ongoing expansion of the rail network in London and its gradually extending suburbs. This fifth edition dates from around 1892 and is notable for the increased detail given to streets and railways compared to the earlier

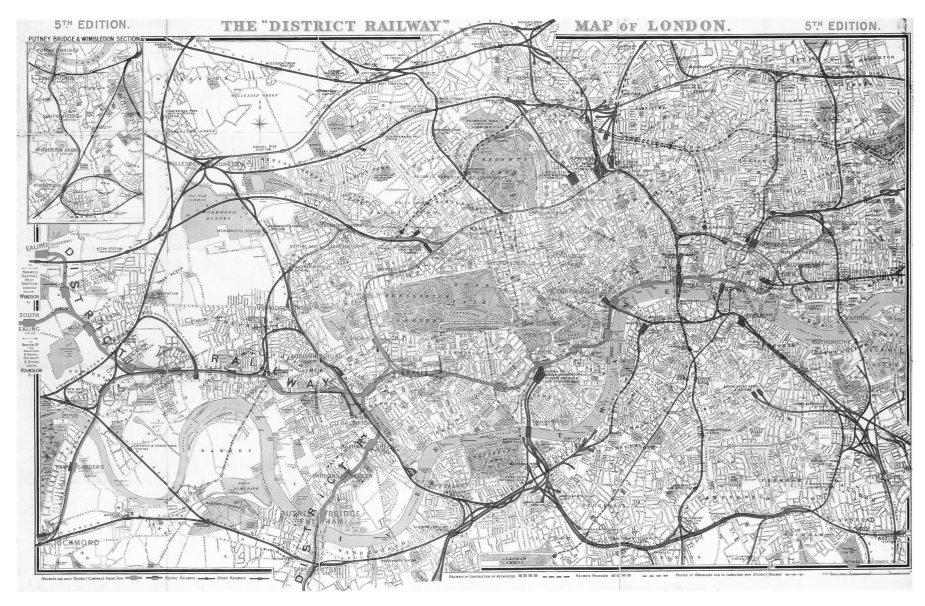

maps in the series. W J Adams was the publisher and printer and it was sold for one shilling (5p) a copy.

More detail and clarity has been given to the street layout and railway routes compared with earlier maps.

The physical area shown has shifted from Westminster and the City forming the centre of the map to a more westward bias, to include new branches being opened west of London: to Richmond (June 1877),

Ealing Broadway (July 1879), Hounslow (March 1883) and Wimbledon (June 1889).

The Inner Circle is now shown complete, the final link between Mansion House and the Tower having opened in October 1884.

This map was one of the first to show the City & South London Railway, which had opened in December 1890 between King William Street, in the City of London, and Stockwell.

This original tube line now forms part of the City branch of the Northern Line. Shown in blue, there may have been some discussion as to whether it should be included at all since it did not operate full size trains. It was possibly treated in this different way for very much the same reason that Bartholomews included some interurban tramways on their road and rail maps while not including urban street tramways, well into the 1950s.

Inside the cover (*left*) are given details of the various presentations in which the map was produced. They are listed *in either book or sheet form as follows:–*

Book Copies.
IN STRONG LINEN WRAPPER;
MOUNTED ON LINEN, IN STRONG LINEN WRAPPER – *Suitable for Libraries, Clubs, Hotels, Public Buildings, &c;*

Sheet Copies.
UNMOUNTED – *Suitable for Engineers'*

and general Office purposes, &c;
MOUNTED ON LINEN – *Suitable for Engineers, Surveyors, &c;*
MOUNTED ON ROLLERS AND VARNISHED – *for the Walls of Offices, Club Rooms, Hotels, Public Buildings, &c.*

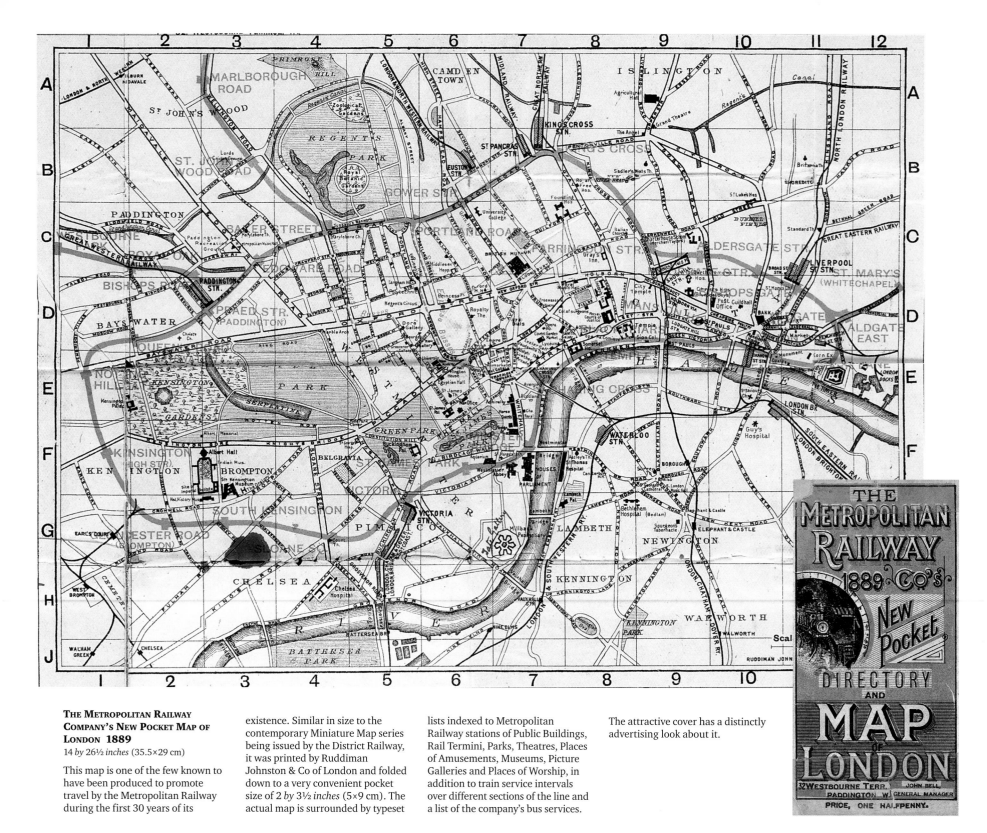

THE METROPOLITAN RAILWAY COMPANY'S NEW POCKET MAP OF LONDON 1889

14 by 26½ inches (35.5×29 cm)

This map is one of the few known to have been produced to promote travel by the Metropolitan Railway during the first 30 years of its existence. Similar in size to the contemporary Miniature Map series being issued by the District Railway, it was printed by Ruddiman Johnston & Co of London and folded down to a very convenient pocket size of *2 by 3½ inches* (5×9 cm). The actual map is surrounded by typeset lists indexed to Metropolitan Railway stations of Public Buildings, Rail Termini, Parks, Theatres, Places of Amusements, Museums, Picture Galleries and Places of Worship, in addition to train service intervals over different sections of the line and a list of the company's bus services.

The attractive cover has a distinctly advertising look about it.

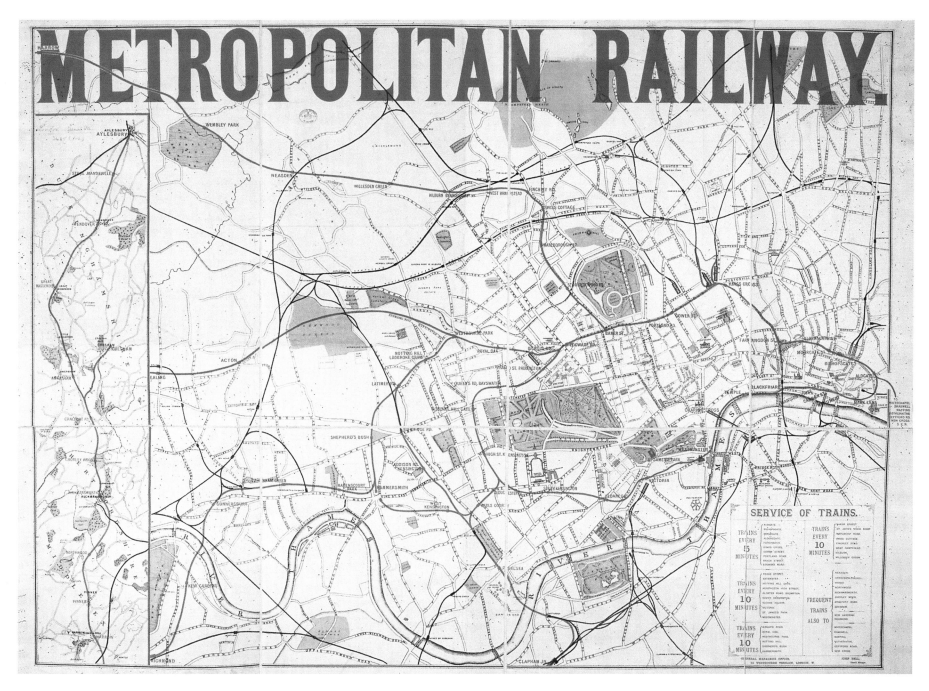

METROPOLITAN RAILWAY c.1894
46 by 33 inches (117×84 cm)

This rare poster style map was mounted on fabric and produced by the Metropolitan Railway around 1894. The style of the streets is very similar to that used by the District Railway for their maps over the previous 20 years.

The railways appear as much finer lines than had hitherto been used on pocket maps, possibly because the size of this map allowed for more fine detail.

Whilst London and its suburbs to the west and north are shown, the other important extension – that into Buckinghamshire which opened two years earlier – is shown in the inset. An indication of the service intervals of trains is also included.

Of interest is the omission of the City & South London Railway (opened in December 1890) although all other railways are included.

Two bus services connecting Charing Cross with Baker Street and Portland Road stations are shown as dotted lines.

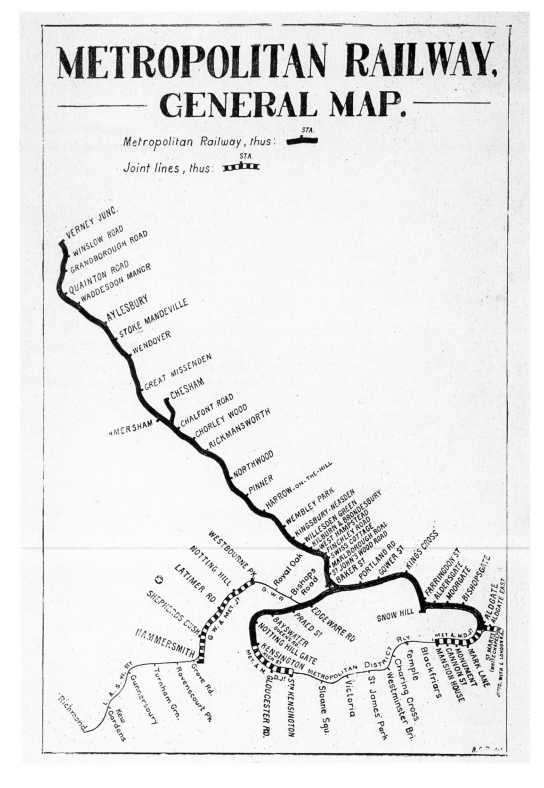

MAP OF THE METROPOLITAN RAILWAY showing stations from Verney Junction in the north down through Aylesbury, Amersham, Rickmansworth, Harrow-on-the-Hill, Baker Street and into the central London circle connecting Richmond, Hammersmith, Kensington, Victoria, Westminster, Blackfriars, Mansion House, Aldgate, Bishopsgate, Moorgate, Farringdon St, King's Cross and Portland Rd.

METROPOLITAN RAILWAY GENERAL MAP c.1898
20¼ by 15½ inches (51.5×38 cm)

It is thought that this map went with a guidebook although this example was issued separately. In contrast to the District Railway, the Metropolitan Railway produced little illustrative publicity during the latter part of the nineteenth century. This map is unusual in that topographical features are not shown – just the Metropolitan Railway, plus its joint and connecting lines. Geography has been distorted to fit in the full extent of the railway out to Verney Junction (except the branch to Brill) – not unusual since some main line railways were altering the shape of Britain on contemporary maps to accommodate their systems.

Having gained control of the Metropolitan, he could put into practice his dream of linking his native industrial Manchester with Kent and the continent of Europe through a tunnel under the English Channel. Although his dream was only to materialise when the tunnel was opened over a century after his company started digging, it does explain the Metropolitan's interest in pushing out toward Buckinghamshire to join with the MSLR which was building southward.

Whilst cool relations between the Metropolitan and the District had been responsible for delaying the completion of the Inner Circle (to the point when Parliament had to make threatening noises) and also the fact that both were not at all prosperous financially, questions were asked if all parties might not benefit if both lines merged. That both railways' relations had degenerated over a considerable period goes some way to explaining why the suburban rail system was built as an unbalanced network of competing lines, each vying to attract traffic from the established trunk railways onto their own system, for onward dispatch to the City. Indeed, Sir Edward exposed the Metropolitan's rift with the District when replying to a suggestion made by an MP in 1876: "This line is doing well – and has nothing to gain – tho' the public may have, by a union". The antagonism between the two was all the sharper since the District enlisted James Staats Forbes as its Chairman in 1872. Forbes was also Chairman of the London Chatham & Dover Railway, which was in direct competition with Watkin's South Eastern for continental traffic.

Rivalry in west London became rife. The Metropolitan, following the District, reached Richmond in 1877, by running its trains over part of the Hammersmith & City and joining the London & South Western line at Addison Road from a junction at Latimer Road. The service only lasted three months, but does show how services were speculated for short periods over 'friendly' companies' lines, in the hope that they could beat the competition and pay their way.

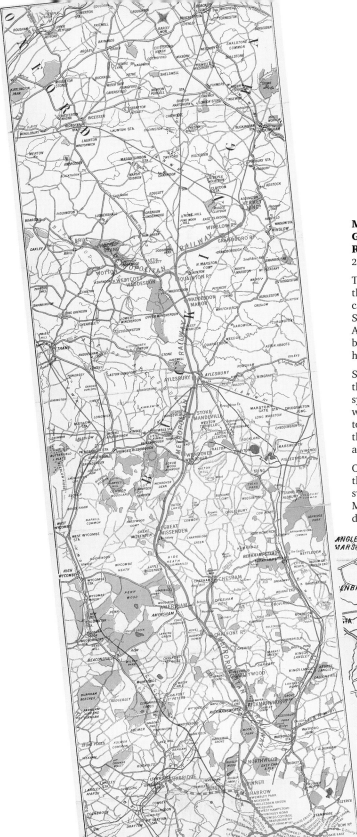

METROPOLITAN RAILWAY CYCLISTS' GUIDE OF CIRCULAR TOURS AND ROAD MAP 1903

26¼ by 8 inches (66.5×212.5 cm)

This map, at first sight, looks to be of the standard style as drawn by the cartographers at the Ordnance Survey, Bacons and Bartholomews. Although this folder was produced by Waterlows, the map itself may not have been drawn by them.

Starting at the bottom, it is then seen that the Metropolitan Railway's system (including the River Thames) within London has been positioned to the north of where it actually is, as though it has been lifted from another project.

On the bottom left, as indicated by the north symbol, the map has been swung right over so that the Metropolitan Railway makes its way directly up the paper. Conspicuous by its absence is the Great Central Railway's line through Gerrards Cross and Beaconsfield to High Wycombe, and between Princes Risborough, Ashendon and Grendon Underwood (the section built in conjunction with the Great Western Railway following the hostile relations that had developed with the Metropolitan Railway). The Great Western line is also missing north of Princes Risborough, perhaps because of its considerably faster service between London and the Brill area.

Less understandable is the deletion of the Oxford to Cambridge line east of Verney Junction, since this must have generated some passengers for Winslow, which has kept its station.

This is a useful map, showing to scale, north of Harrow, the full extent of this urban railway with main line aspirations.

The back of the map contains the cyclists' routes in diagram form, together with very detailed lists of hotels that can be stayed at – the equivalent, one hundred years ago, of today's motoring holiday touring Europe!

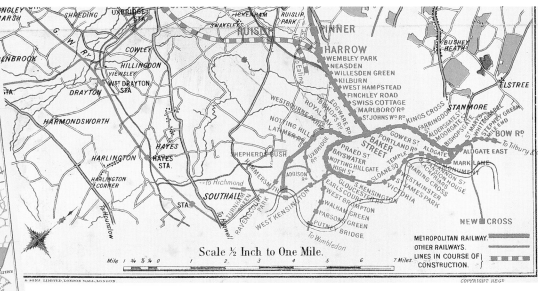

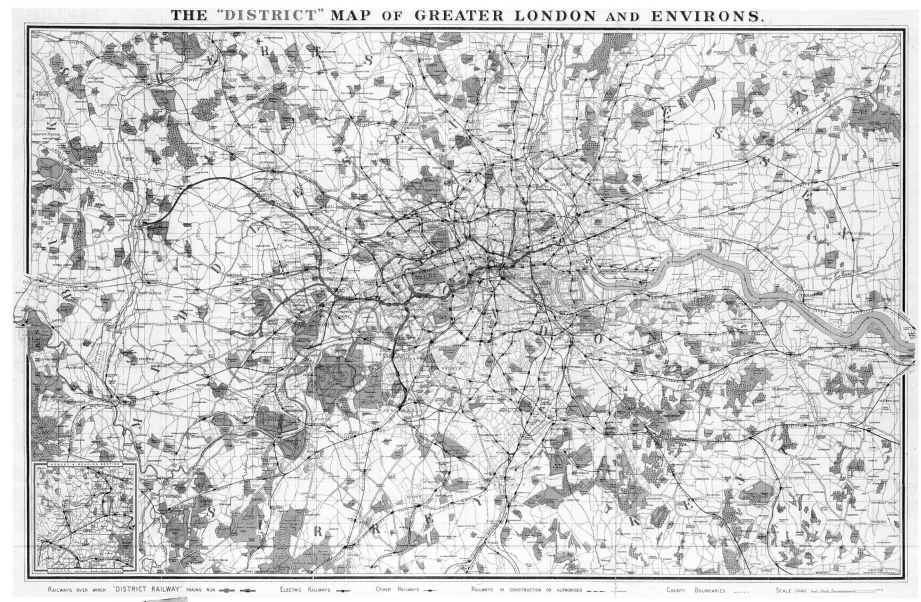

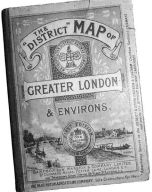

THE "DISTRICT" MAP OF GREATER LONDON & ENVIRONS C.1905

42 by 26¾ inches (108×68 cm)

This large and detailed map was published in various editions by Sampson Low, Marston & Company, known today as the publishers of *All the World's Railways*.

Inside an attractive cover (*left*), the map embraces a massive area of London and its outer suburbs from Windsor to Brentwood and from Purley to Borehamwood. This means that the area of central London looks congested, particularly with the inclusion of new and soon to be opened tube railways.

In addition to tracing the route of the District Railway, such is the detail, it could have been the standard map of London and its environs to be kept in every suburban household.

The District Railway, and those lines over which its trains ran, are shown in red. Other lines are shown in blue with rectangular shaped stations, except those served by electric trains which are shown with circles.

New lines included are those to South Harrow, opened in June 1903, and the Metropolitan Railway from Harrow-on-the-Hill to Uxbridge, opened in July the following year.

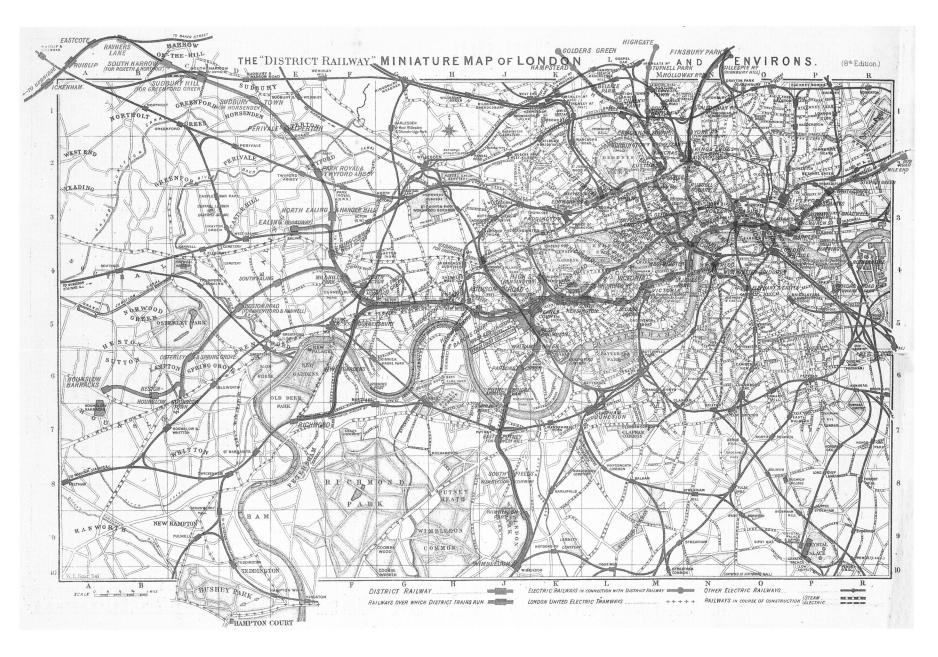

THE "DISTRICT RAILWAY" MINIATURE MAP OF LONDON & ENVIRONS 1908

17¼ by 11¼ inches (44×29 cm)

The District Railway had produced this smaller sized edition since the early 1890s. This version of early 1908 folds down to a convenient pocket size of 2¼ by 4 inches and was probably produced by Waterlow & Sons.

As the area of London included on the map continued to grow, the detail shown here has become extremely congested.

By the time this map was issued, the District Railway was under the ownership of the Underground Electric Railways Company of London, as were the three most recently opened tube railways. All are shown in red on this map, while other railways appear in black. The final map in the series, issued around 1921, shows all lines in red.

The back of this little folder is brimming with travel information and prices.

METROPOLITAN RAILWAY 1910

19½ by 15½ inches (49×39 cm)

From its opening in 1863, the Metropolitan Railway had produced little cartographic material which was aimed for general use by travellers. However, this map of 1910 is an example of a style which had been utilised by the District Railway for many years in its miniature map series. Printed on paper and folded into eight, the main face covers the central districts of London, with the Metropolitan and its connections in red and all others in blue. In contrast to its contemporaries issued by the Underground Group, this map persists with the inclusion of a street plan as a background.

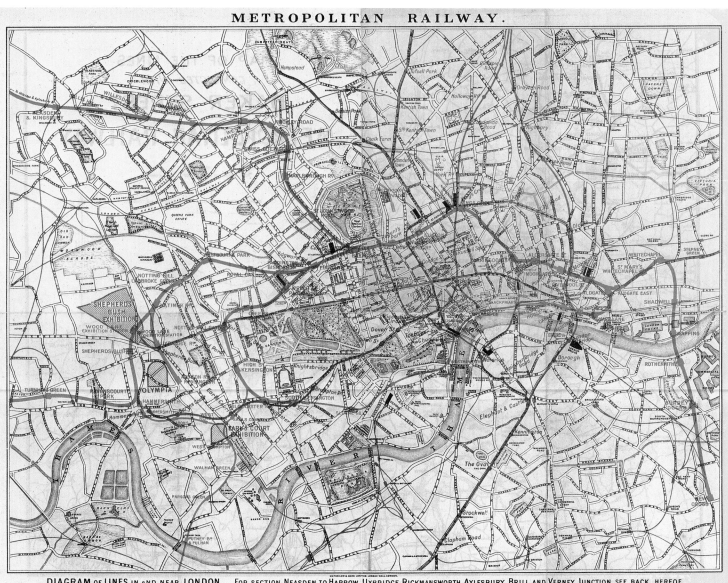

The reverse side is perhaps of equal interest, for it depicts the entire Metropolitan Railway from the City and Baker Street to its remote terminal at Verney Junction, and Brill – less than eight miles from Oxford! Only two short suburban additions were to bring the railway to its full extent, those to Watford in 1925 and Stanmore in 1932, before contraction began in 1935 under LPTB ownership.

Maps of this style were to be found inside Metropolitan Railway timetable publications until the late 1920s.

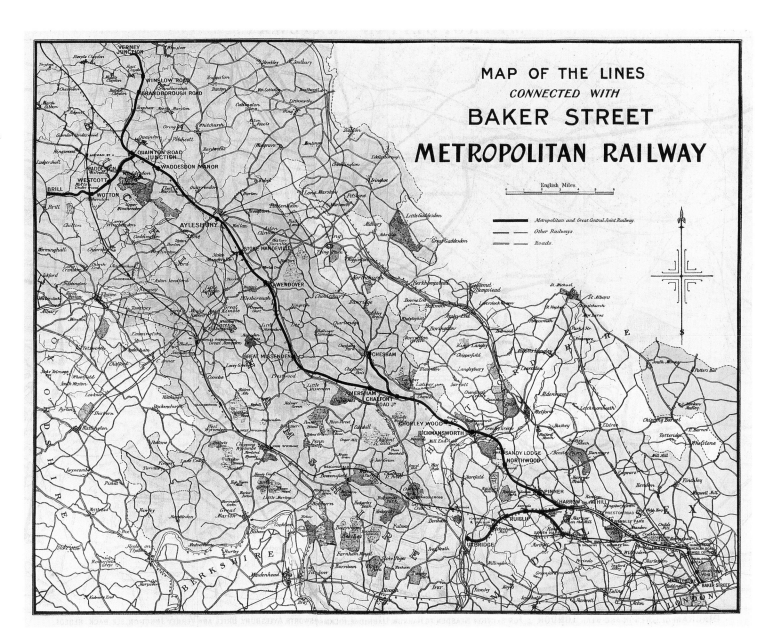

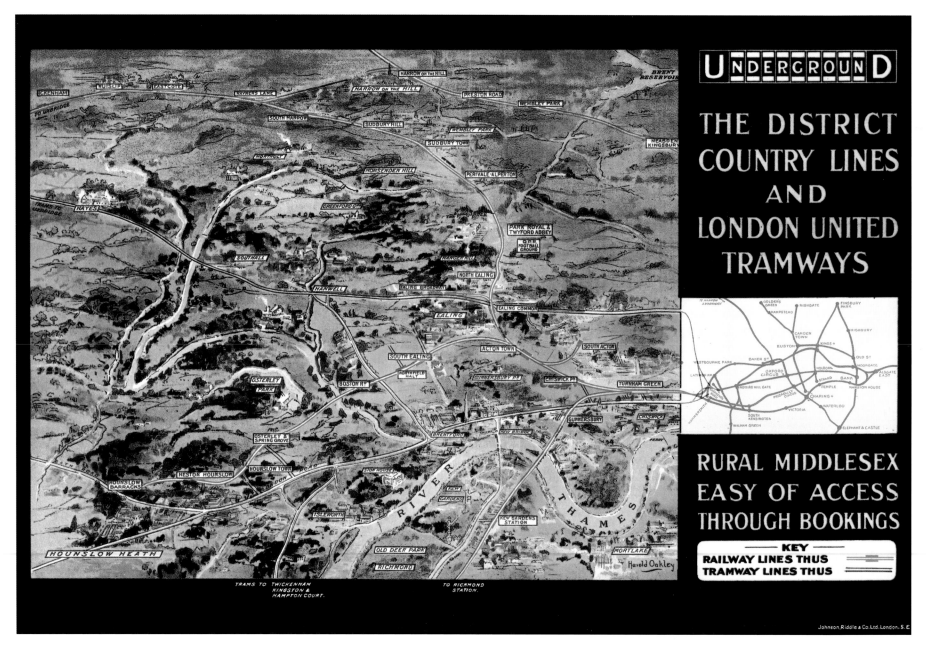

UNDERGROUND

THE DISTRICT
COUNTRY LINES
AND
LONDON UNITED
TRAMWAYS

RURAL MIDDLESEX
EASY OF ACCESS
THROUGH BOOKINGS

KEY
RAILWAY LINES THUS
TRAMWAY LINES THUS

THE DISTRICT COUNTRY LINES AND LONDON UNITED TRAMWAYS 1910

14½ by 9¾ inches (37×25 cm)

The District Railway was as keen to carry Londoners out to the country as it was to take its suburban customers into central London. By the time this folder was issued the London United Tramways had been electrified for ten years and the District for five, thereby creating a unified and progressive system of transportation in south west London. The area west of London is shown from a bird's eye view to emphasise its greenness. Water abounds and the scene has a similarity, and appeal, to a style employed by the Swiss to depict the Alps. The rail lines are joined cleverly onto a map of central London lacking both background and perspective. The artist's name is Harold Oakley and it is probable that the printer, Johnson Riddle & Co, commissioned him to do the work.

METROPOLITAN RAILWAY AND CONNECTIONS c.1924

9 by 6½ inches (23×17 cm)

Unlike the map of 1898, on page 18, which showed only the Metropolitan lines, this map includes routes on the Underground Electric Railways as hatched lines, mainly to show easy connections from the West End and south London. The East London

Railway is shown as solid since the Metropolitan was a part owner, with the LNER and Southern Railway.

The similarity in style to the 1898 map is apparent, in that topographical features are not included. One innovation is the logical treatment of interchange stations by solid circles, the white centres drawing attention to their

special status as opposed to the solid circles of ordinary stations.

Locations of the various housing estates are prominently shown, which Metropolitan Railway Country Estates Ltd had, from 1919, speculatively built for sale, ideally to commuters into London. On absorption of the Metropolitan into the LPTB in 1933, the Country

Estates company was left out of the scheme, to be allowed to continue building houses to feed the railway.

The 'main line' ends, coincidentally, close to where the Metropolitan line terminates now, at Amersham, since stations beyond to Aylesbury, Verney Junction and Brill are not shown.

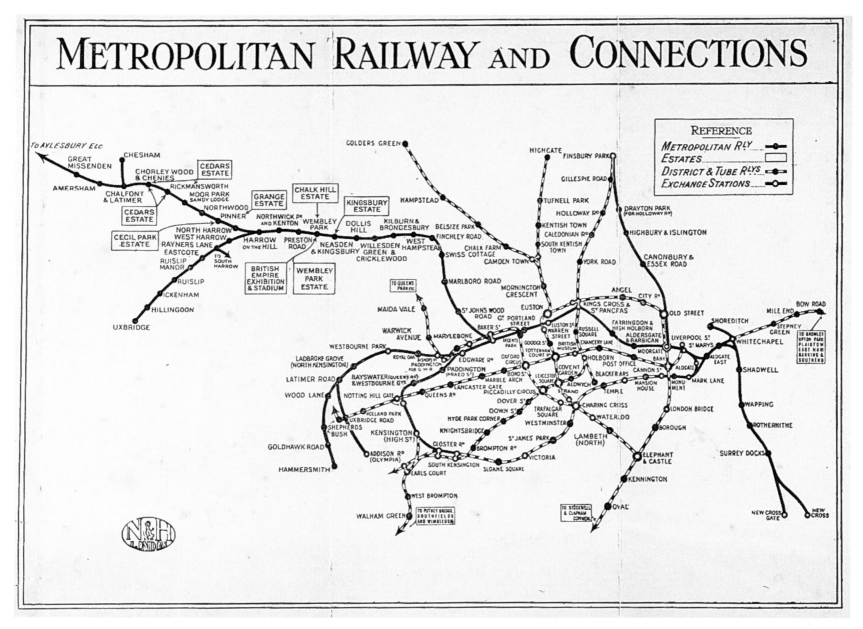

METROPOLITAN RAILWAY AND CONNECTIONS 1924

5¾ by 4¼ inches (15×11 cm)

The Metropolitan Railway produced this small folder map in 1924 and 1925 in a similar format to those issued by London Electric Railways from the mid 1920s. It was produced in order to publicise the convenience of the Metropolitan route to Wembley and the British Empire Exhibition as the cover makes very clear.

Whilst being of bold approach, the thick lines completely swamp the station names which, in many cases, have had to be squeezed in. The roads are so rudimentary that there seems little point in their inclusion as they merely add to the clutter.

A similar map was reissued regularly in a larger paper format until the Metropolitan Railway lost its independence in 1933, when incorporated into the London Passenger Transport Board.

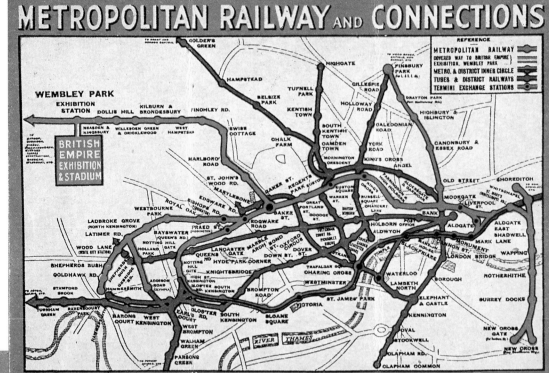

Main Line Stn.	Connecting Station	Remarks
Paddington ...	Praed Street (Metro.)	Subway
	Bishop's Road (Metro.)	Covered wa
Marylebone ...	Edgware Road (Metro.)	3 min. wall
	Baker Street (Metro.)	5 min. wall
Euston	Euston Square (Metro.)	5 min. wall
St. Pancras ...	King's Cross (Metro.)	1 min. wall
King's Cross ...	King's Cross (Metro.)	Subway
Liverpool St. ...	Liverpool St. (Metro.)	Subway
Broad St. ...	Liverpool St. (Metro.)	1 min. wall
Fenchurch St. ...	Mark Lane (Metro. and District)	3 min. wall
	Aldgate (Metro.) ...	5 min. wall
Cannon Street ...	Cannon Street (Metro. and District)	Subway
London Bridge ...	Monument (Metro and District)	3 min. wall
St. Paul's ...	Blackfriars (District)	Covered wa
Charing Cross ...	Charing Cross (District)	Short walk
	Trafalgar Sq. (Bakerloo)	Short walk
Waterloo	Waterloo (Bakerloo)	Covered wa
Victoria	Victoria (District) ...	Subways

"METRO." ROUTE TO AND FROM THE MAIN LINE RAILWAY TERMINI

The Metropolitan Railway—the World's Pioneer Underground System — provides the easiest, quickest and best route to the British Empire Exhibition. Its Train Service is unequalled for frequency and rapidity, its directness of route is unrivalled, whilst the convenience and comfort provided by the system are its outstanding features.

The "Metro" provides direct and speedy access with all parts of the Metropolis; it links up at eight points with London's Tube System, and affords an exceedingly convenient system of connection with the whole of the Main Line Termini.

A special Exhibition Station has been erected at Wembley Park, including a COVERED WAY DIRECT INTO THE EXHIBITION GROUNDS.

HOW TO GET TO AND FROM THE BRITISH EMPIRE EXHIBITION, WEMBLEY PARK.

UNDER COVER ALL THE WAY   UNDER COVER ALL THE WAY   UNDER COVER ALL THE WAY

The Metropolitan Railway's entrance to Gloucester Road station was adjacent to that of the District Railway. This late 1920s picture shows the Metropolitan Railway's answer to the bullseye with its red diamond, still to be seen on station façades at Farringdon (adjacent to the 'parcels office') and Willesden Green, where a clock version is also preserved.

METROPOLITAN RAILWAY AND CONNECTIONS

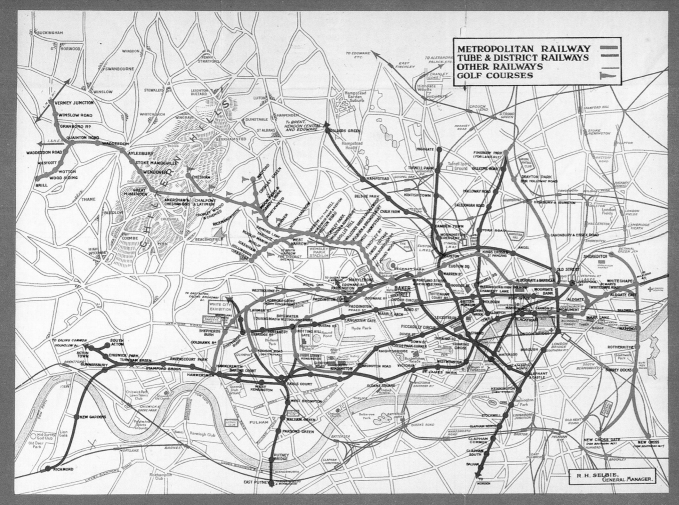

Map legend:
METROPOLITAN RAILWAY
TUBE & DISTRICT RAILWAYS
OTHER RAILWAYS
GOLF COURSES

R.H. SELBIE, General Manager.

ALSO SEE KEY MAPS OF THEATRES, RAILWAY TERMINI, PLACES of INTEREST &c. ON REVERSE SIDE

METROPOLITAN RAILWAY AND CONNECTIONS c.1928

17 by 13½ inches (44×35 cm)

This map is one in a series that was to develop over a decade from the early 1920s until 1933, forming the standard Metropolitan Railway folder map over the period. Compared with the 1924 map opposite, the lines have become much finer, have shed their outlines and now balance the station names. Metropolitan Railway lines are in red, all Underground lines in blue, whilst main line railways are also acknowledged in the background. All railways that were outside the Met's sphere of operations are excluded – even details of rail connections with Verney Junction and Quainton Road are missing. The roads do no more than provide a background. But there is definitely an 'Underground' influence in the overall treatment.

The entire Metropolitan network is displayed in a clever distortion of geography – a fitting memento of an independent railway that was soon to become a memory.

The cover design for this series was within what had become a house style, with the treatment of the railway's name and use of typefaces which had become common to many of the Metropolitan Railway's publications.

METROPOLITAN RAILWAY

MAP OF LONDON

EXTENDING TO DISTRICTS SERVED BY THE METROPOLITAN RLY IN MIDDLESEX, HERTS AND BUCKS

BAKER ST STATION N.W.I.   R.H. SELBIE GENERAL MANAGER

Chapter 3 Early electric railways

Charles Tyson Yerkes

Conditions encountered when riding behind steam locomotives within tunnels were dingy in the extreme. First class compartments were almost empty, the occupants for whom they had been provided preferring to use their own horse drawn accommodation through the streets, while second and third class were packed with office clerks and workmen respectively who had no other choice.

By the 1880s, more underground railways were being promoted to link the suburbs of London with the City. These were of little consequence to the Metropolitan and District since they were intended to serve areas which were well away from their sphere of intense competition. One line was the City & South London, running between Stockwell and the City at King William Street. It opened in December 1890 and could have been treated as an isolated and never to be repeated case of Victorian entrepreneurialism. Its tunnels were deep below the streets, with platforms connected by lifts to the street level booking office. Trains were tiny, with minute windows just below the roofs of the carriages: for who wanted to gaze through a window onto the side of a tunnel?

However, it was electricity that powered the locomotives that hauled the trains and illuminated the interiors of cars and

GREAT NORTHERN, PICCADILLY & BROMPTON Ry. MOTOR CAR.

Locomotives caused excessive vibrations to the buildings above, so future trains were built with their motors in part of the leading and trailing cars, thereby spreading the adhesion. This type of car was used when the Great Northern Piccadilly & Brompton Railway opened in 1906.

stations. Thus there were no steam and oily smells on London's first tube. Indeed, the air was often fouler at street level, when it is remembered that every vehicle – buses, trams, lorries, hackney cabs – was propelled by horse; within London, in 1909, the tramway companies alone possessed 25,000 horses!

The success of electricity provided the spark that was to inspire the development of the next tube, the Waterloo & City Railway which was to open in 1898. Its carriages had normal size windows and the interiors were spacious within their small dimensions. This short line of 1½ miles (2.4 km) was built with the financial assistance of the London & South Western Railway who nurtured it as a cheaper link with the City instead of extending their own line from Waterloo, with the inevitable demolition of property on both sides of the River Thames. Full integration was formalised when the LSWR took complete control from 1 January 1907.

Then came the Central London Railway, in 1900, from Shepherd's Bush to Bank and running under the entire length of Oxford Street. Also electrically worked, a standard fare of 2d was charged for a ride of any distance. This quick, clean, cheap and direct little tube brought the lumbering, oppressive, slow and smelly Metropolitan and, especially, the hard pressed District, to their knees. The two railways were already considering electrification of their lines, but had to agree on a common system to work the Inner Circle, and their established animosity was making agreement virtually impossible. Of the situation in which the Metropolitan and District Railways found themselves, the *Railway Magazine* of February 1902 quoted a certain Mr Yerkes: "Here were a lot of men, who called themselves business men, in charge of railroad property, sitting by and seeing the Central London Road (*sic*) being built. When the Central London really opened, and their trade began to fall away, they did not even move then, but sat and looked further, and have continued to do the same ever since".

Charles Tyson Yerkes was the entrepreneur from Chicago who had rescued the financially troubled District a year

In addition to the maps forming publicity, others were specially printed to accompany official documents – many to a technically high standard of cartography.

In 1884, Henry Greathead (designer of the famous tunnelling shield that still bears his name) and others obtained powers to construct a cable driven tramway system in twin tunnels between the north side of London Bridge and Elephant & Castle. Known as the City of London and Southwark Subway, construction commenced in May 1886 and authority was received to extend the line south to Stockwell a year later. In August 1888, the momentous decision was made to convert from cable traction to the largely untried use of electricity. Thus, two years later on 4 November 1890, the world's first electrically operated deep tube railway was opened under the new title of the City & South London Railway.

This map dates from the mid-1880s and shows the route of the subway beneath Newington Causeway and Borough High Street. The locations of the three stations which were to serve the line are clearly shown, but none was originally planned to serve London Bridge main line station. Of interest are the tramways, which would then have been horse drawn, and the other railways including what later was rebuilt to become the Thameslink line with its northerly junction to both Farringdon and Aldersgate (now Barbican) stations. It was litho printed by Standidge & Co of Old Jewry in the City.

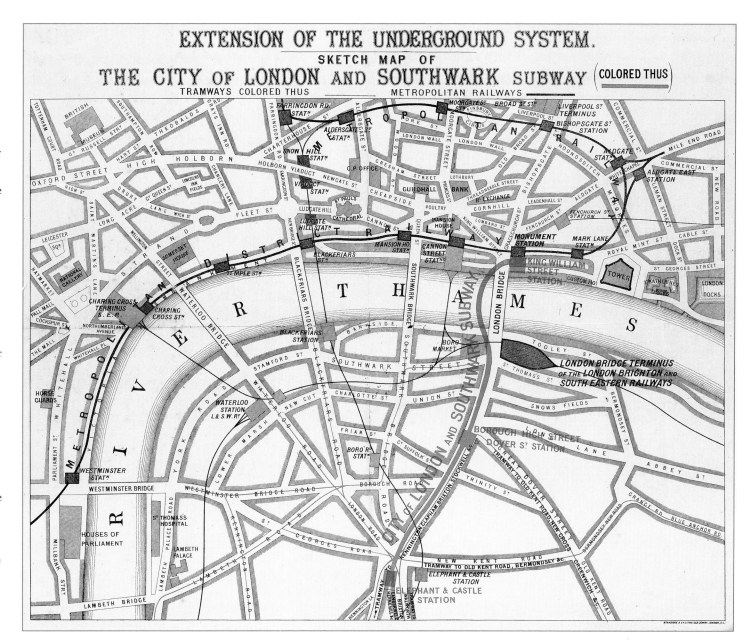

before. He brought with him a quarter of a century of experience in the operation of urban railways and tramways, in later years using electricity for their propulsion. He also brought vast financial resources. Having bought control of the District Railway in 1901, he then set up the Metropolitan District Electric Traction Co Ltd to effect the electrification and also reduce the tension with the Metropolitan, so that both could agree on the same electrical system. Tube lines which

were presently being promoted or built, two being the Brompton & Piccadilly Circus and the Great Northern & Strand (which were to form the nucleus of the present Piccadilly Line), were acquired. His finance also allowed the moribund Charing Cross Euston & Hampstead (now part of the Northern Line) and the Baker Street & Waterloo (the Bakerloo) tubes to continue to be built.

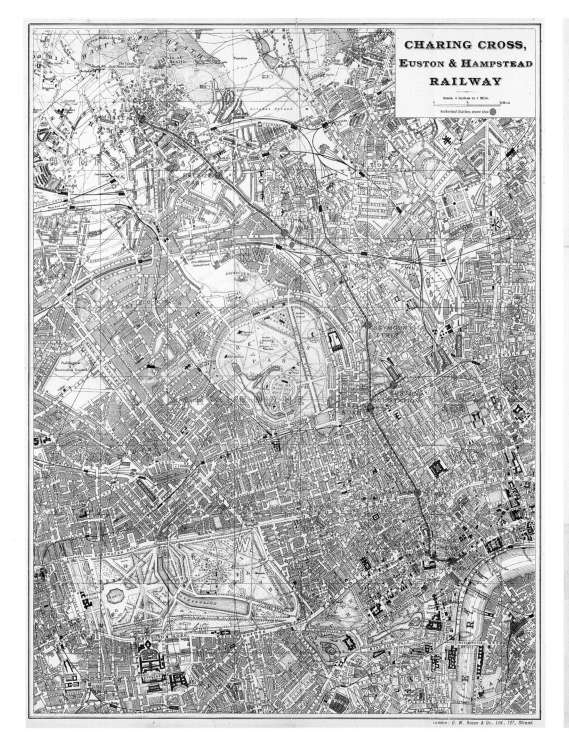

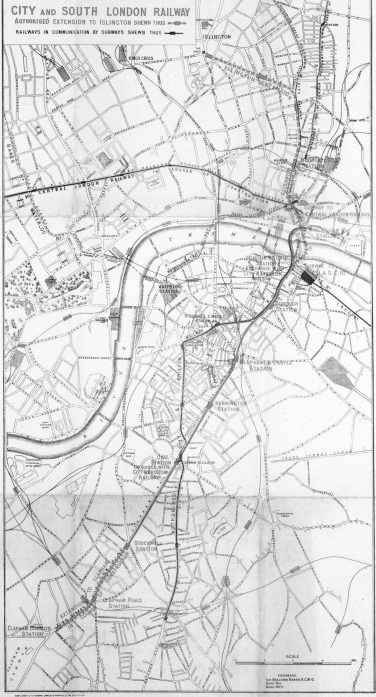

CHARING CROSS, EUSTON & HAMPSTEAD RAILWAY c.1898
(*far left*)
16¼ by 20¾ inches (41.5×53 cm)

In 1892, a Parliamentary Bill was deposited to construct a railway between Hampstead High Street and the south end of Charing Cross Road, with a branch to the north of Euston Road to serve King's Cross and St Pancras main line stations. Royal Assent was granted in August 1893 for the newly named Charing Cross, Euston & Hampstead Railway, but withheld for the branch to King's Cross. Further Bills sought powers to extend south to Charing Cross and north to Golders Green, with a branch to Highgate.

This map, produced by G W Bacon from their standard street plan, may have been used to accompany the 1898 Bill which sought to realign the southern section of the line so that it terminated under 23 Craven Street to the west of Charing Cross SER station. The map shows this change but not a revised course between Euston Road (Warren Street from 1908) and Seymour Street (eventually to open as Mornington Crescent), which allowed Euston station to be placed on the main route instead of the terminus of a short branch line. No reference is made to stations that were to open at Leicester Square or Goodge Street, while Camden Town is indicated by a broken circle only. The line opened on 22 June 1907.

CITY & SOUTH LONDON RAILWAY c.1899 (*left*)
14 by 24½ inches (36×63 cm)

This latter-day use of an engraved map was produced by J Cook & Hammond, better known now as Cook Hammond & Kell of Mitcham. This map shows the location of King William Street, the original northern terminus when the line opened in December 1890. It also illustrates the trajectory the new portion of line would follow from north of Borough station towards Islington, so avoiding King William Street which was approached along a sharp

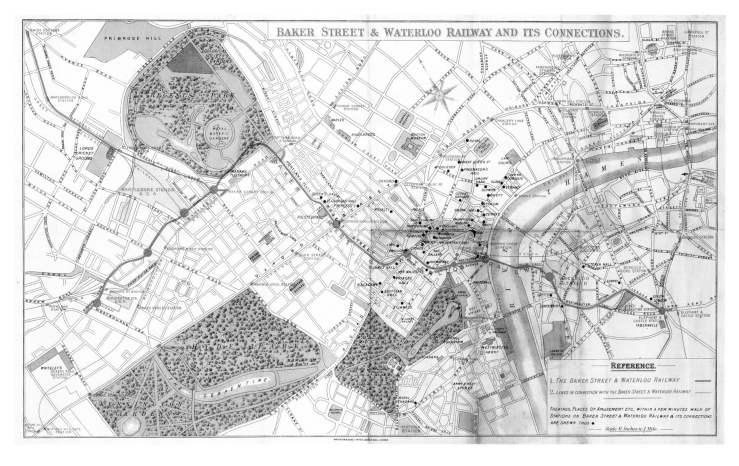

inclined curve, severely restricting the line's capacity. This was opened as far as Moorgate Street (Moorgate from 1924) in February 1900, and Angel in November 1901. To the south, the extension from Stockwell to Clapham Common opened in June 1900.

The route is also shown of the proposed Brixton Extension Railway, which would have utilised the soon to be abandoned King William Street curve and terminus. This line was never built, which may have been due to the electrification of the LCC tramways running at street level along the same route. The course of the Central London Railway, then under construction, is show boldly, probably because it would have direct interchange with the CSLR and did not pose any competition.

BAKER STREET & WATERLOO RAILWAY AND ITS CONNECTIONS c.1899 (*above*)
29 by 17 inches (51×26.5 cm)

Another Bill was deposited at the 1892 session for a line from Baker Street via Regent's Street and Charing Cross to Waterloo for which assent was granted in March 1893. Powers were obtained three years later to extend the line from Baker Street to the proposed London terminus of the Manchester, Sheffield & Lincolnshire Railway (to become Marylebone of the Great Central Railway).

Although tunnelling commenced in 1898, exact details of the course of the line were still undecided, for a further Bill was submitted in 1899 seeking powers to build two extensions – one to Paddington (to the west of the GWR station), the

other a branch from Regent's Park to Euston. While this Bill was rejected following opposition from the Metropolitan Railway, a revised version, covering extensions to Paddington (Bishop's Road) and Elephant & Castle, was granted Royal Assent in 1900.

This map probably accompanied the 1900 Bill, for it illustrates the two extensions, the subway link into the GWR station and the (as yet unnamed) Edgware Road station. At this time, no reference is made to stations at Regent's Park or Lambeth North, which were not to be authorised for a further four years. The alignment of the railway to the west of Edgware Road was later abandoned when it was decided to extend the line northwards beyond Paddington in 1915.

A study of the Waterloo & City

Railway also merits attention. Although the line opened in August 1898 between Waterloo and City (now Bank), the City terminus is shown as Royal Exchange, which is located to the east of its current site and appears to serve jointly with the Central London Railway, which was to open two years later. An intermediate stop on the WCR is indicated at Mansion House, which became the site of the actual terminus, with a pedestrian link to the CLR's ticket hall at Bank (Royal Exchange).

Several CLR stations were to have had different names – Newgate Street (Post Office, then St Paul's), Bloomsbury (British Museum) and Westbourne (Lancaster Gate).

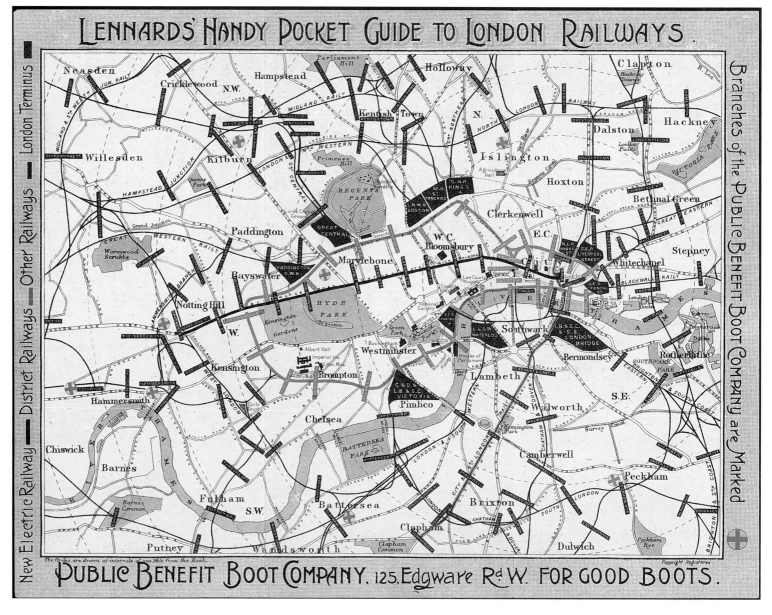

**LENNARDS' HANDY POCKET GUIDE TO
LONDON RAILWAYS c.1900**
10¾ by 8¼ inches (27.5×21 cm)

Publishers have always been aware of the commercial possibilities of street plans of London and, with lithographic methods becoming readily available to printers towards the end of the nineteenth century, the use of bold areas of colour became possible. This map combines the finesse of engraving of the

background with the boldness of solid blacks and reds to indicate railways and stations.

A novel feature is the positioning of station names across their lines, which might necessitate twisting the map at angles to read them. Another feature of this map is the depiction of the Central London Railway as a 'New Electric Railway' in juxtaposition with the Inner Circle (credited as being the District

Railway) which, useful as it was, had its rather grubby trains hauled by smelly steam locomotives.

The City & South London Railway had been open for over ten years at the time of the appearance of this map and so had probably lost some of its novelty appeal. It is therefore not shown in the same bold form. The Central London Railway's Post Office station (renamed St Paul's in 1937) is shown as Newgate Street –

a name that it never adopted. The main line terminal stations cover such an area (to accommodate their names) that King's Cross, St Pancras and Euston stations appear next door to each other. The other locations prominently marked on this map are the premises of the Public Benefit Boot Company, sponsors of this publication.

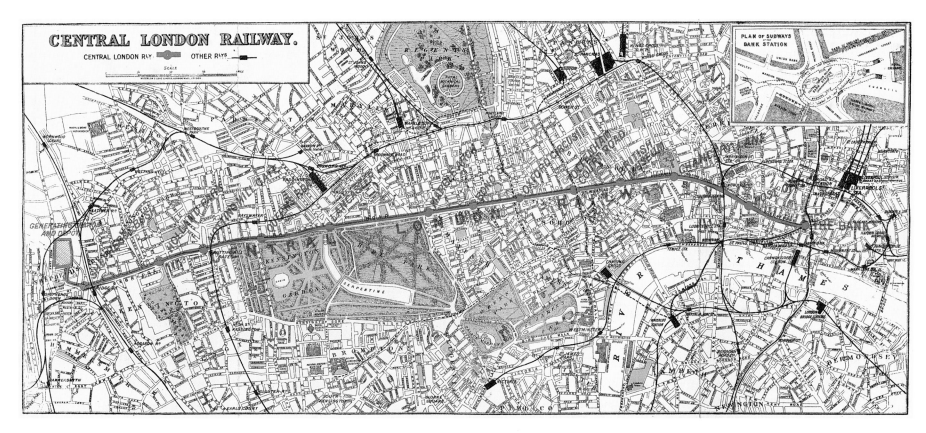

CENTRAL LONDON RAILWAY c.1902

12¾ by 5¾ inches (32.5×15 cm)

The opening of the City & South London was followed, in July 1900, by that of the Central London Railway between Shepherd's Bush and Bank, running in tunnels driven beneath Bayswater Road, Oxford Street and High Holborn. Its opening was accompanied by a new form of map which was to be commonplace until the 1930s. The publication consisted of a street layout printed on paper and folded into four, with travel information on the reverse side. Thus this was perhaps the first truly pocket map of an Underground line.

The route of the Central London Railway is shown as a red line overlaid on the street background, while other railways are not highlighted in any way. The inset plan of the subways around Bank station is a particular feature of this series of maps, dating from the early 1900s.

The Central London Railway was always keen to show its proximity to the well known attractions of London and this map shows them well – the parks and even the River Thames at Bank all look to be within walking distance. A very detailed map, but at the same time appearing clear, possibly because the detailed background is so regular as to act as a tint. The traffic generated by the City was very important to the CLR's success.

On the right is Oxford Circus station shortly after it opened, as depicted on a contemporary postcard. This building still survives at the junction of Argyll Street and Oxford Street.

C. L. R. Twopenny Tube.　　　　*Oxford Circus Station.*

GREAT NORTHERN & CITY ELECTRIC RAILWAY 1904

8¼ by 15¾ inches (19×38 cm)

This map appears to have been issued for the opening of the "largest and best tube railway in the world" in February 1904. The line was so described because, while the construction followed the methods employed by the City & South London and Central London railways, the tunnels were large enough to accommodate full size trains. The Great Northern & City Railway is shown in a bold red, while those companies with which agreement had been made to sell combined tickets – the City & South London, Great Northern and London Brighton & South Coast railways as well as the Metropolitan Electric Tramways (which ran extensive services from Finsbury Park) – are in blue. Other lines are in black, with the Central London Railway appearing slightly bolder.

This map is unusual in adopting a portrait format, thereby conforming with the north-south orientation of the line. Printing is by McCorquodale & Co Ltd, another of the railway orientated specialists.

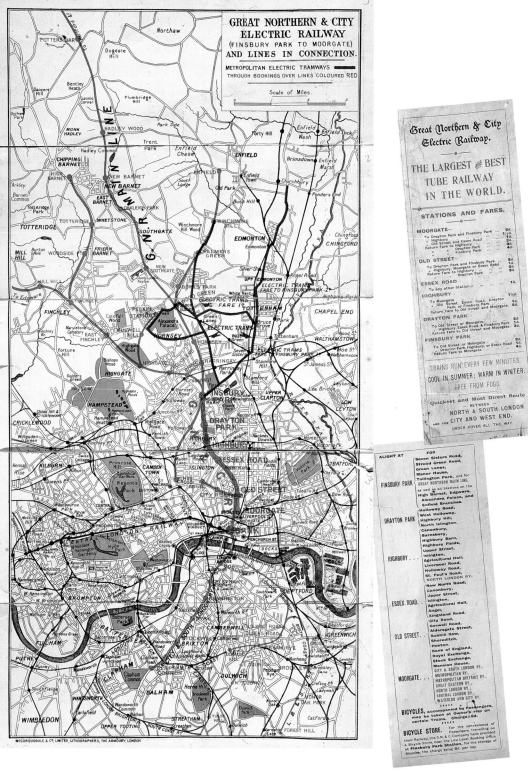

34

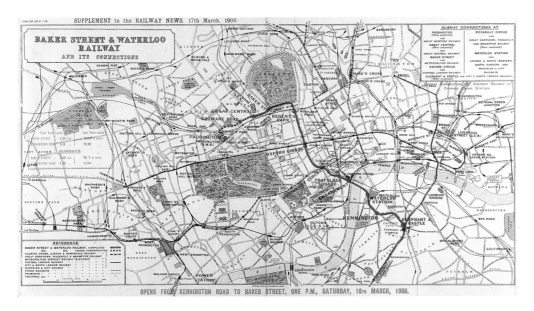

BAKER STREET & WATERLOO RAILWAY AND ITS CONNECTIONS

OPENS FROM KENNINGTON ROAD TO BAKER STREET, ONE P.M., SATURDAY, 10th MARCH, 1906.

BAKER STREET & WATERLOO RAILWAY
AND ITS CONNECTIONS 1906

16 by 9 inches (40.5×23 cm)

There is a certain similarity between these maps and the 1902 folder of the Central London Railway, possibly because all were produced by Waterlow & Sons. By the time the Baker Street & Waterloo Railway opened in March 1906, it too had

been integrated into the Underground Group which meant that there were advantages if it and the other railways in the group could all be shown on its map.

The top map was printed exactly a week after the railway's opening and was issued as a supplement to the *Railway News*. The station known as Lambeth North since 1917 was to be

named Kennington but was renamed Kennington Road for the opening, and again to Westminster Bridge Road on the extension of the railway to Elephant & Castle (shown as already open) in August 1906.

Main line railways which were also thought to be able to generate passengers for the underground railways are shown in bold black, while others that might be in competition are in thin black.

Selected complementary bus and tram routes are also shown (the associated London United tram routes being given a special red treatment).

The publishers of the lower of these two maps, which dates from late 1906, showed confidence in the

builders by quoting opening dates of not only their own extension to Paddington, but also of two other railways – such optimism persisting between operators and builders to this day. As events turned out Great Central (Marylebone since 1917) opened in March 1907 and Edgware Road opened in June 1907 (the line reached Paddington in 1913).

It was also in the year that these maps appeared that the Evening News newspaper, through their diarist 'Quex' (Captain G H F Nichols), allegedly coined the portmanteau name 'Bakerloo' in place of the cumbersome title of the railway, the name being officially adopted by the company in July 1906.

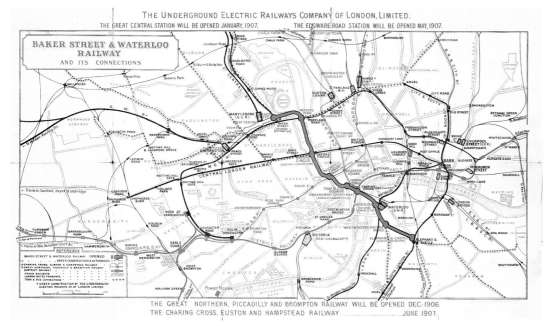

THE UNDERGROUND ELECTRIC RAILWAYS COMPANY OF LONDON, LIMITED.
THE GREAT CENTRAL STATION WILL BE OPENED JANUARY, 1907.   THE EDGWARE ROAD STATION WILL BE OPENED MAY, 1907.

BAKER STREET & WATERLOO RAILWAY AND ITS CONNECTIONS

THE GREAT NORTHERN, PICCADILLY AND BROMPTON RAILWAY WILL BE OPENED DEC. 1906.
THE CHARING CROSS, EUSTON AND HAMPSTEAD RAILWAY   JUNE 1907.

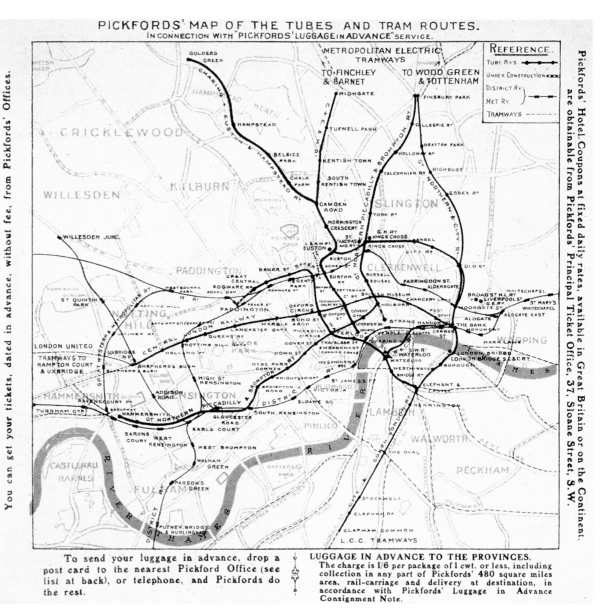

PICKFORDS' LONDON RAILWAY PLAN
1907

5 by 4¾ inches (39×21.5 cm)

Among the headaches of travel across the country through the heart of London are the changes necessary from one main line terminus to another. Luggage causes another obstacle and it is often easier to take a taxi ride instead of negotiate the intricacies of the Underground.

Pickfords came to the rescue with this convenient leaflet offering their services to look after your luggage for the entire journey and give help for you to get from one side of London to the other.

All lines are shown in black, although differentiation is made between tube lines, those under construction, the Metropolitan and District railways, and tram routes. The cover is notable for its strong red background, its illustration and the inclusion of a reference code.

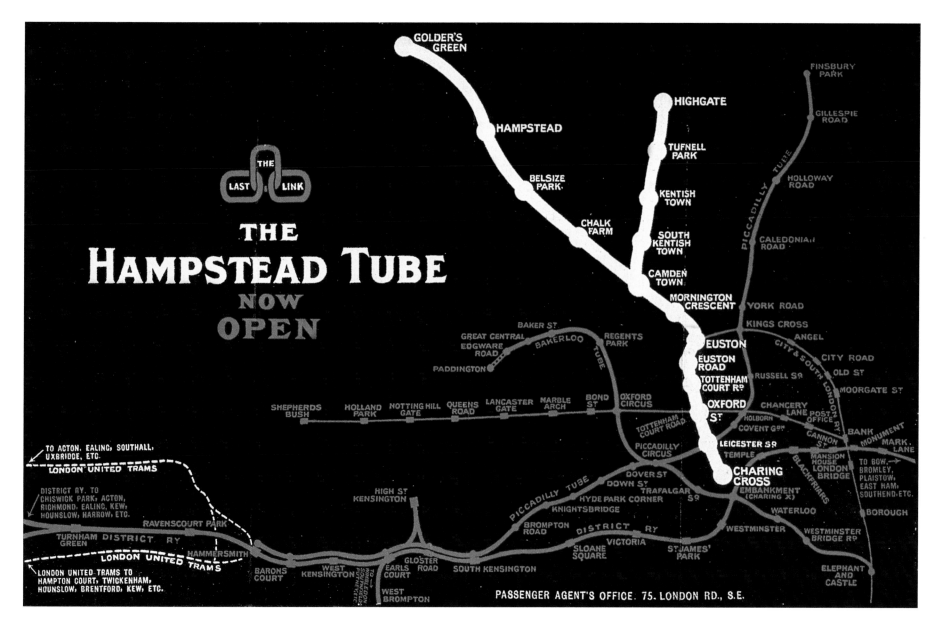

The Hampstead Tube Now Open
1907

9¾ by 6 inches (25×16 cm)

This map was produced by Johnson Riddle & Co, probably in their studio, for the opening in June 1907 of the Charing Cross Euston & Hampstead Railway. Its unique representation bears little semblance to previous maps, many of which owed their design to the engraved maps of the nineteenth century. Only those lines forming part of the

Underground Electric Railways Company are shown plus (as thinner lines) the Central London and City & South London railways. While geography has been distorted, it still has not eased the problem of visual confusion that was becoming apparent in the area covering Holborn and the City.

A confusion of conflicting station names can be seen: the CCEHR chose to call its station Oxford Street (to entice the shoppers), while the

Central London named theirs Tottenham Court Road. The CCEHR conformed the following year and renamed its own Tottenham Court Road to become Goodge Street.

Interestingly, stations on the Hampstead, Piccadilly and Bakerloo railways are shown as circles, while those on other railways (including the Underground's own District Railway) are shown as rectangles. The motif above the title celebrates the fact that this opening formed the

culmination of the Underground Group's project to complete the construction and inauguration of train services on its three tube railways within 15 months.

The CCEHR was given the name 'Hampstead Tube' from the start, hoping to follow the popularity that the Bakerloo name enjoyed. When it was merged with the City & South London Railway, in 1926, the name 'Morden–Edgware' was applied to the combined line. The name was

changed again in 1937 to the 'Northern Line' to reflect the extensions being built to the north of London.

The Hampstead Tube was determined to lure tram passengers from northern suburbs onto its trains, rather than let them travel the entire way by tram between their suburban homes and central London.

37

CENTRAL LONDON RAILWAY 1908
(cover below)
11¼ by 7 inches (28.5×18 cm)

The opening of the Franco-British Exhibition on a large site, which included White City Stadium, a short distance to the north-west of the Central London Railway's depot, led to an extension being built from the existing terminus of the railway at Shepherd's Bush to a new station at Wood Lane. Both the station and the exhibition that it served opened in May 1908. Later that year the station widened its role when the White City Stadium became a venue for the Olympic Games.

SOUVENIR LONDON ELECTRIFIED c.1908 *(left)*
3½ by 5½ inches (9×14 cm)

This map, issued as a postcard, was produced as a private commercial venture. It will be seen that tube railways only are prominently featured, whether owned by the Underground Group or not. Hence, the District and Metropolitan railways are reduced to thin pecked lines without intermediate stations (except Lords) and without their extremities defined as enjoyed by the tramways. The Met fails, even, to gain recognition in the key.

While the Anglo-French Exhibition (known elsewhere as Franco-British) of 1908 is featured with its own little motif, there is no reference as to where it is – presumably the designer was not aware that the Central London Railway was extending its line from Shepherd's Bush to Wood Lane to serve the exhibition when it opened.

An interesting treatment of the station names, which anticipated that used on some Stingemore maps 20 years later, was to colour the lettering to match the lines. Tottenham Court Road on the CCEHR is to the pre-1908 configuration, while the Oxford Street name is missing. Lastly, the Tower of London appears to be on the wrong side of the River!

HOW TO GET TO THE IMPERIAL INTERNATIONAL EXHIBITION 1909 *(right)*
12 by 9 inches (30.5×23 cm)

The Metropolitan Railway produced this map the following year to promote its services to the White City exhibition site. The layout has been somewhat simplified, with the omission of part of the Piccadilly line and many of the stations on this and the other 'tube' railways. No reference is made whatsoever to the Central London Railway or to its station adjacent to the Met's own on Wood Lane, for this line represented the greatest competition for exhibition traffic. Some aspects of topography have been distorted quite significantly, such as the compression of the Uxbridge branch and the expansion of the Hammersmith and Addison Road lines so that they appear to terminate south of Earl's Court!

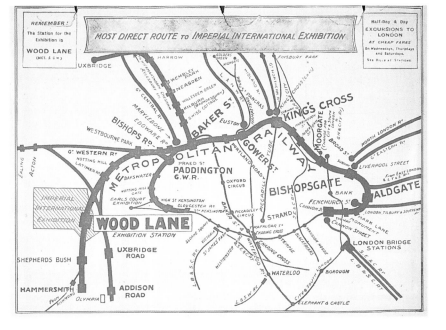

38

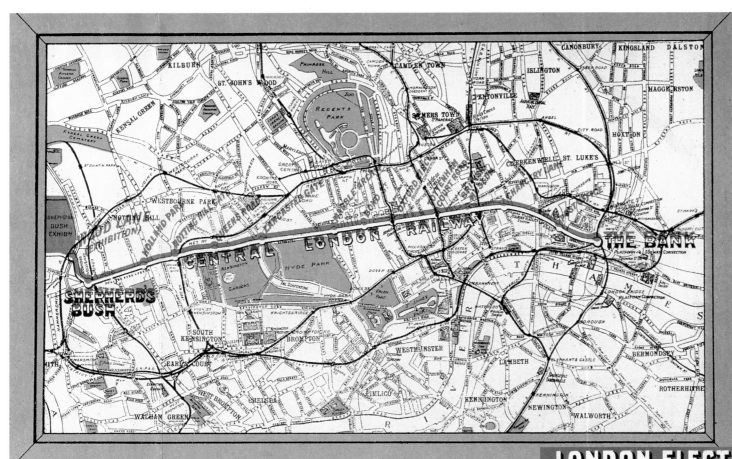

CENTRAL LONDON RAILWAY c.1909
11¼ by 7 inches (28.5×18 cm)

The map on the cover side is similar to, but not as detailed as, the map produced for the railway in 1902 (*page 33*). The earlier version had the line and station names simply overprinted in red. It is possible that the letterpress plates for this map were sent from Waterlows to Johnson Riddle who printed this folder, hence the similarity with the earlier map.

This version has the line and terminal station names as well as the line name in red with a black shadow, with the unfortunate effect seen here. It is not unusual for this type of leaflet to be seen with similar *out of register* printing. The bad registration of the red extends also to the back cover.

The map on the reverse side appears to have been a standard London Electric Railways version supplied to all printers of folders for their subsidiary companies. This was probably the result of the historic meeting chaired by Lord Ashfield in 1907, in which he also offered the use of the bar and red disc symbol to any operator of urban railways within London.

Hence, on this map, all lines are given equal prominence (except, strangely, the East London Railway since the District Railway had an interest in it). This appears to be the first instance of each line being given a distinctly different colour – the two lines to retain their colours to this day being the District and the Baker-loo (although it did depart from the brown between 1924 and 1933).

The Central London has been given blue, which conflicts with the red used on the cover side and on previous maps where red had been accepted as the line's colour.

Stations with subway connections employ a device very similar to that developed by Henry Beck on his diagrammatic maps after 1933 and still in use today. Of connecting services, the London United Tramways received special treatment since it was already part of the Underground Group. Of all the different tram operators covering the area, only the Metropolitan Electric Tramways receives a mention, while the two other tram lines shown (and many are omitted) have to be content with anonymity.

CENTRAL LONDON TUBE RY. 1910

(*below*)

5½ by 3½ inches (14×9 cm)

At first sight this appears to be a simple postcard promoting the Central London tube. However, blowing into the small hole on the address side inflates the card to a box shape, to reveal photographs of the Japan-British Exhibition being held at Wood Lane.

H Grube Ltd, the printer, also possibly devised this intriguing advertising device as a private venture, since patent number 2856/1910 follows the imprint. This could explain why the map was drawn in this unique style. The Inner Circle has been stretched and the

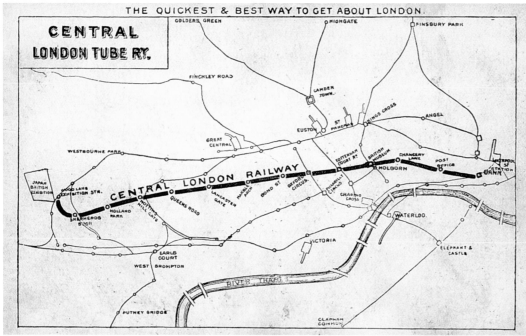

City & South London appears to terminate at London Bridge. The Waterloo & City turns into the District, which itself terminates at Bank. Some interchange stations are shown as diamonds – Camden Town has been accorded a unique status.

The treatment of Central London station circles breaking the thick line is neat and all are given names. But stations on other lines are shown either without names or not at all.

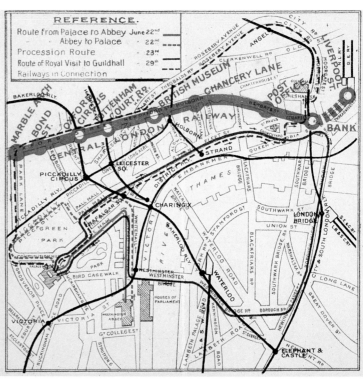

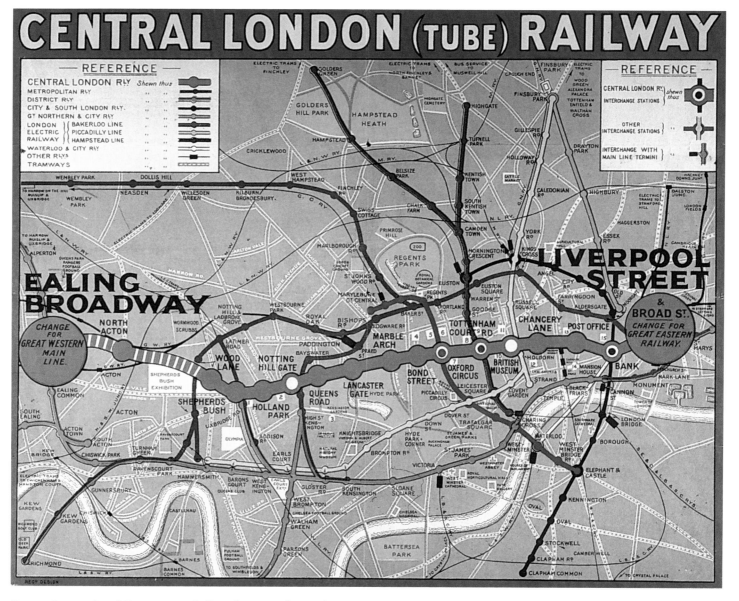

**CENTRAL LONDON (TUBE) RAILWAY
ROUTES OF THE CORONATION
PROCESSIONS 1911** (*left*)

5 by 4¾ inches (13×12.5 cm)

The coronation of King George V was
the first in which the tube railways
could play an important part in
bringing people to the processional
route. The Central London was keen
that it should feature in visitors'
travel plans, by issuing this pocket
map combining the route of the
procession (to which only Bank
station was adjacent) with hints to
shopping and entertainment.

The map on the inside shows the
West End and City portion of the
Central London Railway, as well as
other tube lines in thin black and the
processional routes in relation to
each other. The extension to
Liverpool Street was not to open for
another year.

**CENTRAL LONDON (TUBE) RAILWAY
1912** (*above*)

14 by 11 inches (36×28 cm)

The overall layout of this version,
produced in the spring of 1912,
follows the style set by the London
Underground Electric Railways and
has been adapted for the Central
London Railway. Compared with the
1909 version, red has been revived
as the Central London's line colour
while the red formerly used to
indicate the Metropolitan Railway
has been altered to dark blue.

There is no explanation of the
meaning of the hatched treatment
between Wood Lane and Ealing
Broadway (it was, in fact, under
construction), while the eastward
extension from Bank to Liverpool
Street (where no indication is given
that it was not yet open) was not to
take passengers until the end of July
1912.

In the key the London Electric
Railway is shown as being the
operator of the Bakerloo Line,
Piccadilly Line and Hampstead Line.
This is probably the first reference to
what was formerly called a 'railway'
or a 'tube' being referred to as a Line.

The prominent title, coloured border
and colour coded lines brought this
production visually very close to
maps being produced for and by the
Underground Group companies.

CENTRAL LONDON (TUBE) RAILWAY
RIGHT INTO LIVERPOOL ST. STATION
1912

14 by 11 inches (36×28 cm)

To promote the opening of the extension to Liverpool Street, the Central London produced this folder towards the end of 1912.

A very simplified version of the map produced earlier the same year, its main aim was to show the connections that could be made onto main line trains at Liverpool Street and Broad Street.

Trams could also be taken from Liverpool Street – but none are shown. The outbreak of World War I in 1914 delayed the construction of the extension to Ealing, which did not open until 1920.

The folder was produced by Johnson Riddle & Co who probably drew the map themselves using the January 1912 edition as reference.

This was to be the last map to be produced by the Central London Railway as an independent concern. The following year would see the line come under the financial control of London Electric Railways.

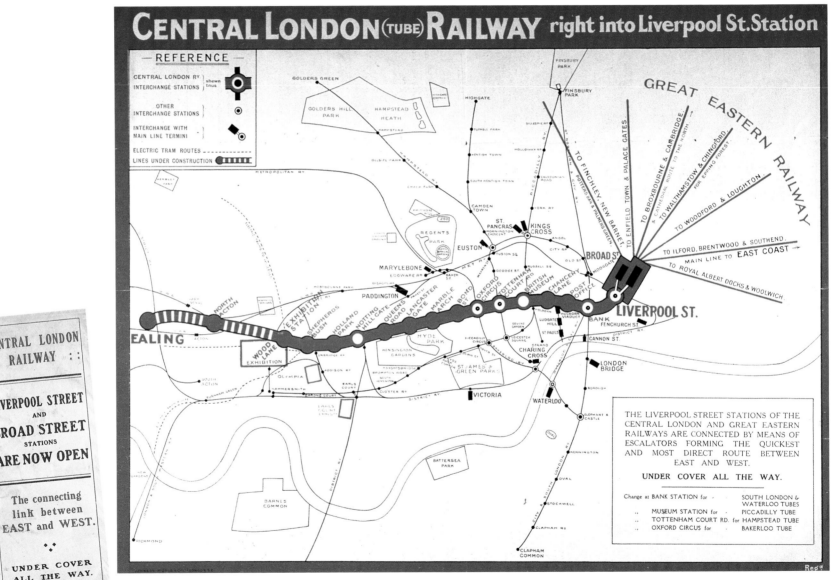

G.N.R. POCKET MAP OF LONDON.

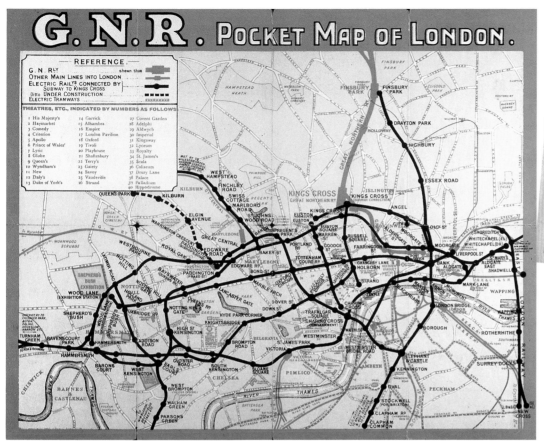

G.N.R. POCKET MAP OF LONDON 1913 (left)

14½ by 11¼ inches (36.5×28.5 cm)

Maps depicting the Underground railways of London were also produced by other railway companies, whose own lines never formed part of the network, but could see the Underground as a marketing asset. This Great Northern Railway map, shows the links from its own services at King's Cross and Moorgate to stations on the Underground.

Electric railways are shown in black, with no distinction between tube and surface lines, whilst main lines running into London (which formed no competition with the GNR) are in red. This explains the absence of the Piccadilly tube between King's Cross and Finsbury Park, which provided a faster – and cleaner – alternative to the Great Northern's steam services serving the same area.

Bakerloo extension stations between Paddington and Queen's Park (which was to open during 1915) show their provisional names: Warrington Crescent (which became Warwick Avenue), Elgin Avenue (Maida Vale) and Kilburn (Kilburn Park).

EAST LONDON ELECTRIFIED RAILWAY AND CONNECTIONS 1915 (right)

7 by 4¾ inches (18×12 cm)

The East London Railway was still an independent company when this map was drawn, although Metropolitan Railway trains had run the passenger services since electrification in 1913, enabling journeys to be made without a change of train between the two lines, which is why both are shown in red.

The style for showing interchange stations anticipated the treatment by Henry Beck on his diagrammatic maps after World War II.

Unusually, no street layout is shown except in east London. This aids the clarity of the map and assists in stressing the connections to main line railways from Liverpool Street, Fenchurch Street and London Bridge.

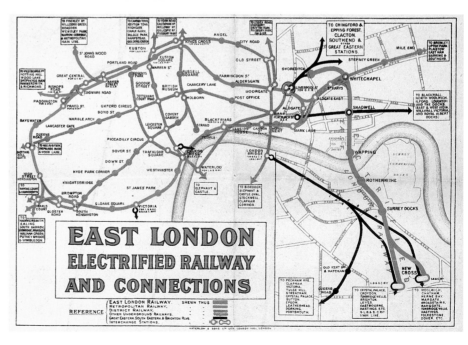

Chapter 4 United we stand

When, in April 1902, Yerkes and a number of financial houses set up the Underground Electric Railways Company of London Ltd, to take over his tube building activities and the Metropolitan District Electric Traction Co, he was positioning the first building blocks of what was later to become London Transport. Being also a tramway man, his interests led him to acquire the London United Tramways Ltd. Based at Hammersmith and Shepherd's Bush, with routes serving Thames-side towns as well as extending the lines to Uxbridge, this recently electrified tram system formed an ideal feeder to the District Railway. The District was also eyeing Uxbridge, opening its line as far as South Harrow in 1903, which was to be London's first electrified line running above ground.

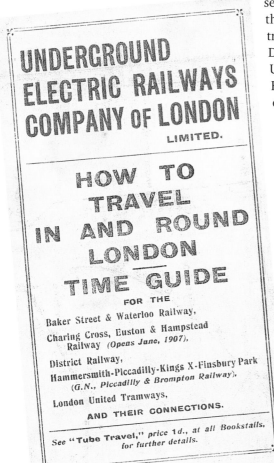

UNDERGROUND ELECTRIC RAILWAYS COMPANY OF LONDON LIMITED.

HOW TO TRAVEL IN AND ROUND LONDON TIME GUIDE

FOR THE

Baker Street & Waterloo Railway,

Charing Cross, Euston & Hampstead Railway (Opens June, 1907),

District Railway,

Hammersmith-Piccadilly-Kings X-Finsbury Park Railway (G.N., Piccadilly & Brompton Railway),

London United Tramways,

AND THEIR CONNECTIONS.

See "Tube Travel," price 1d., at all Bookstalls, for further details.

Electrification was effected on the Inner Circle in 1905, as were the lines connecting with it. The Bakerloo and Piccadilly tubes were brought into use in 1906 and the Charing Cross Euston & Hampstead, with a branch from Camden Town to Highgate (now called Archway), during the following year.

It was also in 1907 that another figure joined the Underground Group from America. Albert Stanley was born in Derby, but spent his early business career in the United States managing public transport in New Jersey. Having found his feet in London, he is credited with the inspiration of a distinctive symbol that could be used to publicise all public transport concerns in London, whether or not they were within the Underground Group (the Metropolitan Railway remained outside until 1933). This was adopted at a meeting of the London Passenger Traffic Conference in February 1908 and took the form of an illuminated red disc bearing the word UNDERGROUND with large initial and final letters. This was to be freely exhibited at all stations, with the Metropolitan adopting a modified version using a red diamond instead of the disc.

This meeting also recommended some changes to station names to avoid confusion to passengers at stations where a change between lines could be made. This ruling, whilst intended to help and encourage passengers holding through tickets from stations on one line to those of another – the Underground was now in competition with the newly motorised buses and electric trams – also helped the designers of maps of the system.

The finances of the Underground Group were still not good. Many people from the former independent companies were finding it difficult to adjust to working in a large corporate group and Stanley was looking around for a strong general manager to weld the force towards the same goal. On Stanley's tours of the offices, one particular young man kept crossing his path, voicing criticisms about the standard of Underground publicity. This young man was Frank Pick and he was working at the time in the office of the District Railway's managing director. Stanley made Pick responsible for the advertising of the entire Underground Group and gave him six months to show some results.

The publicity that Pick had been criticising consisted mainly of simple announcements conveying the sort of information that would be sent to newspaper editors. He noticed that whilst the Company was making a substantial profit from the sale of advertising space at stations, none was being utilised by the Underground itself.

The first poster that Pick commissioned cried 'Underground to Anywhere'. A few days later 'Book here for Central London Railway: New Through Bookings' appeared outside all stations except those of the Central London. Another poster which

UNDERGROUND ELECTRIC RAILWAYS OF LONDON 1907

15 by 11 inches (38×28 cm)

This map is significant in that it was the first to be produced with the title of 'Underground Electric Railways of London' depicting the integrated network formed from the individual operators under its control. Other lines over which the Underground Group's railways had running powers or with which it had working agreements are shown as bold black lines, while those with which it had no relationship (including the Great Northern & City Railway) are shown with thin lines. The Charing Cross Euston & Hampstead Railway had not yet been opened, nor had the Baker Street & Waterloo Railway's extension from Baker Street to Great Central (now Marylebone).

Of the tram routes, as was becoming usual, the LER-owned London United lines are given special status. However, while the Metropolitan Electric in north London and LCC routes in south London are also shown, those in east London are ignored.

This map was printed by Waterlow & Sons.

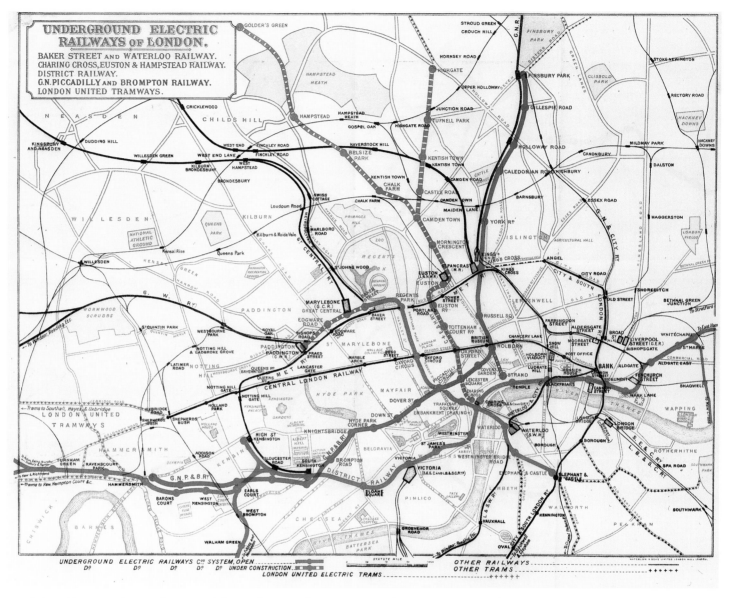

proclaimed 'Four trains per hour to Richmond on Sunday afternoons', with a painting of the Richmond riverside, showed that Pick was wooing the type of leisure traveller that hitherto was probably not already aware of where the trains went. He commissioned John Hassall, a noted and popular commercial artist, to produce a poster for the Underground. His poster (featured on the frontispiece of this book) 'No need to ask a P'liceman' shows an elderly couple, asking a low comedy policeman, who jerks his thumb over his shoulder towards a large Underground map.

The time was now rife to consider developing a corporate Underground system identity, from the red disc and standard name to actually showing the system as a whole on maps. By the time that the first system map was produced by London's Underground in 1908, the only independent lines were the Central London and City & South London railways (which were already concerned about a downturn in passenger numbers), the Metropolitan and the Great Northern & City. The Central London and City & South London railways became part of the Underground Group in 1913.

HAMMERSMITH, PICCADILLY, KINGS CROSS, FINSBURY PARK
(G.N., PICCADILLY & BROMPTON RAILWAY.)

Hammersmith,
Barons Court.
Earls Court.
Gloucester Road.
South Kensington
Brompton Road.
Knightsbridge.
Hyde Park Corner.
Down Street.
Dover Street.
Piccadilly Circus.
Leicester Square.
Covent Garden.
Holborn.
Russell Square.
Kings Cross.
York Road.
Caledonian Road.
Holloway Road.
Gillespie Road.
Finsbury Park.

BAKER STREET AND WATERLOO RAILWAY.

Elephant & Castle.
Westminster
  Bridge Road.
Waterloo.
Embankment—
  Charing Cross.
Trafalgar Square.
Piccadilly Circus.
Oxford Circus.
Regent's Park.
Baker Street.

CHARING CROSS, EUSTON & HAMPSTEAD RAILWAY.

(Open June, 1907.)

Charing Cross.
Leicester Square.
Oxford Street.
Tottenham
  Court Road.
Euston Road.
Euston.
Camden Town.
Chalk Farm.
Belsize Park.
Hampstead.
Golders Green.

Castle Road.
Kentish Town.
Tufnell Park.
Highgate.

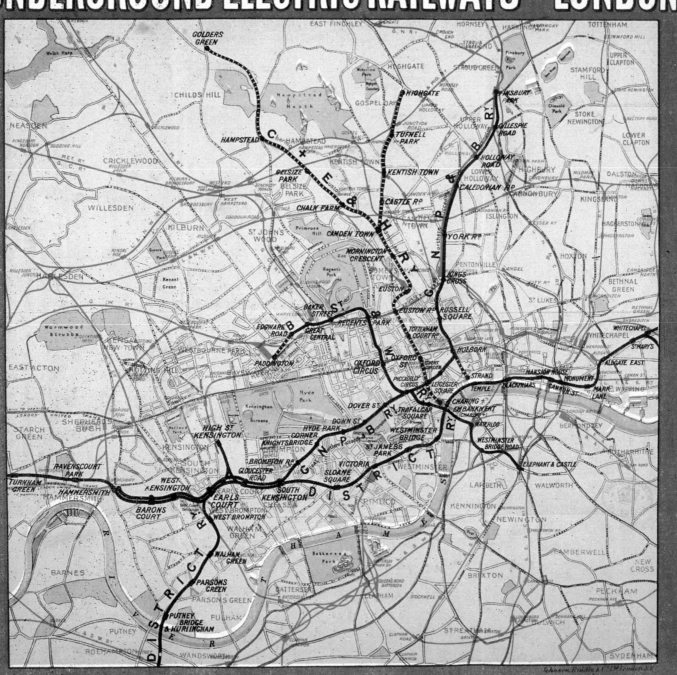

THE DISTRICT RAILWAY.

MAIN LINE.

Ealing Broadway.
Ealing Common.
Mill Hill Park.
Chiswick Park.
Turnham Green.
Ravenscourt Park.
Hammersmith.
Barons Court.
West Kensington.
Earls Court.
Gloucester Road.
South Kensington.
Sloane Square.
Victoria.
St. James's Park.
Westminster.
Charing Cross.
Temple.
Blackfriars.
Mansion House.
Cannon Street.
Monument.
Mark Lane.
Aldgate East.
St. Marys.
Whitechapel.

EXTENSIONS.

South Harrow.
Sudbury Hill.
Sudbury Town.
Perivale-Alperton.
Park Royal.
North Ealing.

Hounslow Barracks
Heston Hounslow.
Hounslow Town.
Osterly and
  Spring Grove.
Boston Road.
South Ealing.

South Acton.

Putney Bridge
Parson's Green.
Walham Green.
West Brompton.

High Street.

This map, with its text running down both sides, was printed by Johnson Riddle & Co, just a few months later than Waterlow's version. The deep green border was to frame most Underground Group maps during the following years. Lines belonging to the Underground subsidiaries are again shown as bold lines. By this time, the Baker Street & Waterloo had opened as far as Edgware Road. Other railways and roads are shown in a detailed, balanced form to the point that the map appears to be a rail and road map of London with Underground routes superimposed.

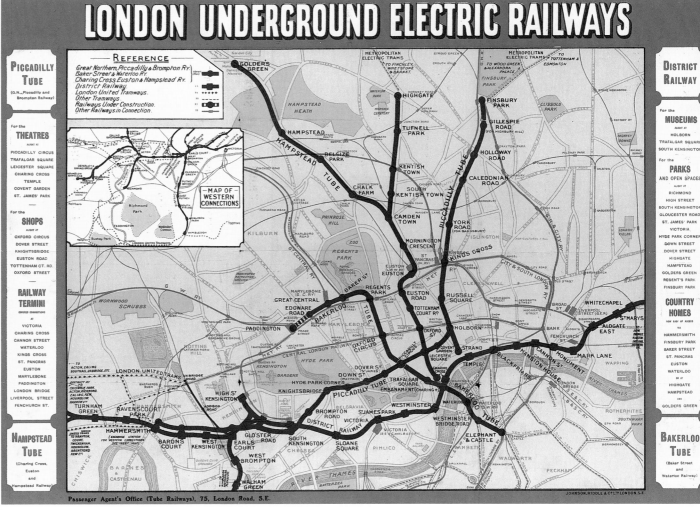

LONDON UNDERGROUND ELECTRIC RAILWAYS 1907
17 *by* 12 *inches* (43×31 cm)

Another version, also printed by Johnson Riddle in 1907, but this time showing the Charing Cross Euston & Hampstead Railway as open. Whilst the full titles of the railways are given in the key, their more digestible idiomatic names are written along the lines on the map. Tube stations are indicated with circles, while those of the District are rectangles. Since stations on the main line railways are indicated in the same way (albeit smaller), it could be that rectangles were used to symbolise railways using main line size trains. The additional line, not owned by the Underground Group and drawn in an intermediate weight, between Earl's Court and Uxbridge Road via Addison Road formed part of the 'Middle Circle' and was also used by London & North Western Railway and later LMS trains until services were suspended in 1940. Uxbridge Road was an important point for catching London United trams. Notice the spelling of 'Gloster' Road.

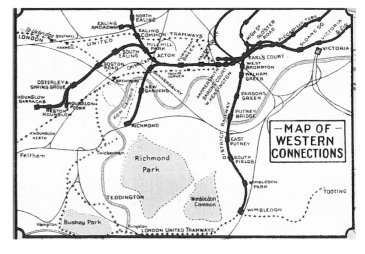

LONDON UNDERGROUND ELECTRIC RAILWAYS 1907 (above)

folded: 5 by 2½ inches (13×6 cm)
open: 14¼ by 2½ inches (36×6 cm)

As the opening of new tube railways gathered momentum, 1906–07 saw the production of large amounts of publicity and advertising material. This is one of a fascinating series of display cards showing a simplified version of an electric railways map and, in the illustration, trackside poster maps.

LONDON UNDERGROUND ELECTRIC RAILWAYS 1908 (right)

14 by 11 inches (36×28 cm)

Using the same artwork as the map produced for the Hampstead Tube opening a year before, this version promotes the District Railway (highlighted in red) and contains only one change: the branch to Strand (known as Aldwych from 1915) is open.

The London United tram routes have been made more prominent. On the inset the District is shown in black, which is strange since it is nearly the same colour as the tram routes.

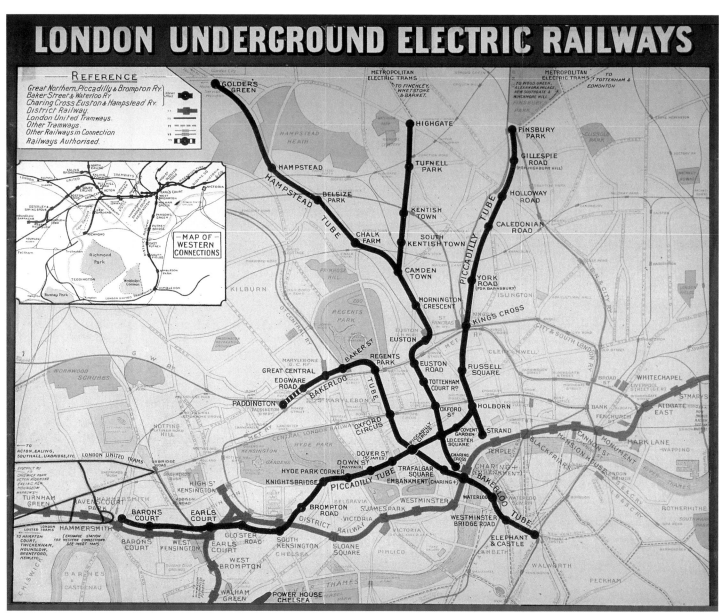

ALL TUBES LEAD TO PETER ROBINSON'S OXFORD CIRCUS 1907 (right)

5½ by 3½ inches (14×9 cm)

This advertising map was printed onto the front of a standard postcard, the back advising the customer that their order was receiving attention by the department store. The title is of interest for its early use of the colloquialism *Tube*, probably on the instigation of the shop itself who may not have been aware of its informality. The map was drawn in the cartographic studio of G.W. Bacon who already had experience of maps depicting Underground lines for inclusion in their guide books.

Only key lines are depicted, with no reference being made to the Metropolitan, City & South London or main line railways. Unusually, for a map of this period, no background detail is shown, adding to its clarity. The Bakerloo Tube extension to Paddington would possibly not have been included if it had been known that it would not open until December 1913.

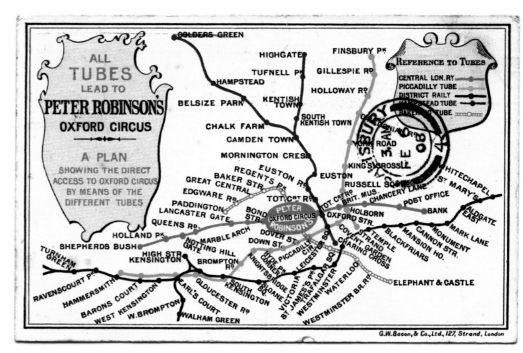

LONDON UNDERGROUND 1908 (left)

5½ by 3½ inches (14×9 cm)

This is the first time that the word Underground was formed into what is now termed a logo, by enlarging the U and D. Waterlow & Sons produced this postcard map, possibly as their own commercial venture, so it may not have been ordered by the Underground Group at all.

A totally different approach to the Underground system, this was a development aimed at advertising the system as opposed to simply offering information. The black background may have been to enhance some of the paler coloured lines, especially those which had always suffered from being indistinct when portrayed on a white background. This approach does allow for a range of distinctive colours which may have merged tonally if they were to be printed darker on a white background.

Thought has been given to the main line stations, with their stubs of line protruding. Meanwhile, the District Railway had to be content with its central portion only featured.

LONDON ELECTRIC RAILWAYS c.1908

14 by 11 inches (36×28 cm)

LONDON UNDERGROUND RAILWAYS c.1908

10½ by 8¾ inches (27×22 cm)

The cartographic element of these two maps is almost identical. However, it is in the border that the front map forms such an important development in graphic design.

This early appearance of the UNDERGROUND logo across the top is significant for it forms an important milestone in the visual portrayal of the Tube map. The feature was to last in this form for over a quarter of a century and, with enlarged initial and final letters, until the mid 1960s.

On the cartographic side, an outline street layout remains, but is of minor prominence compared to the bold representation of the railways themselves. The cartographer has adjusted geography in order to fit the Metropolitan Railway around the key box.

Black outlines have added to the pale colours of yellow and orange to make them more recognisable. The treatment of the yellow with outlines persisted until the 1980s, although it was for the Circle and not for the Piccadilly Line.

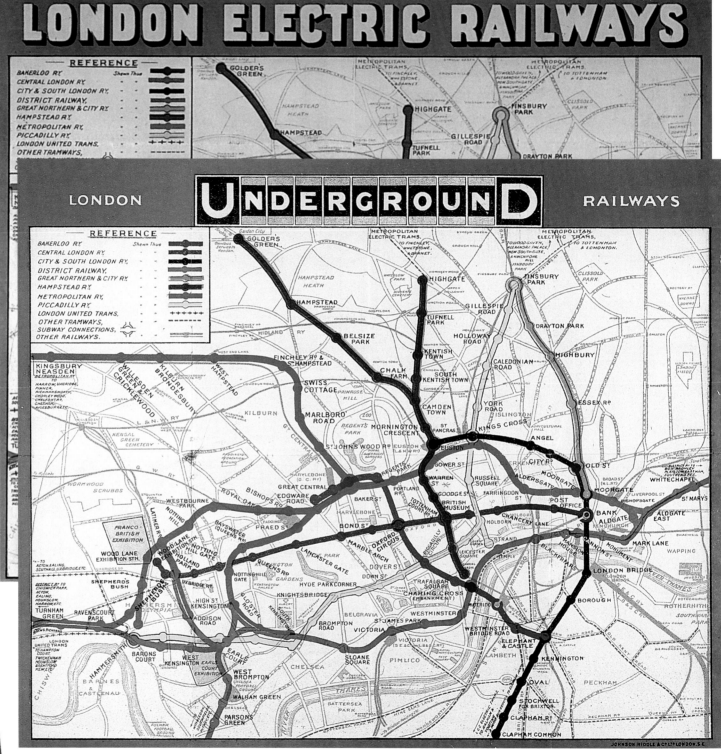

LONDON UNDERGROUND:
ROYAL HORTICULTURAL SOCIETY
1908

10½ by 8½ inches (27×21.5 cm)

This map is superficially very similar to its contemporaries in its style and size.

However, the design has been modified to include extensive reference to what would now be

called a 'sponsor' – in this case the Royal Horticultural Society – giving it a particularly distinctive appearance.

The Society has usurped the title position for their own name, whilst

reference to the Underground is relegated to a corner. An inset map shows the location of the Society's exhibition hall in Westminster.

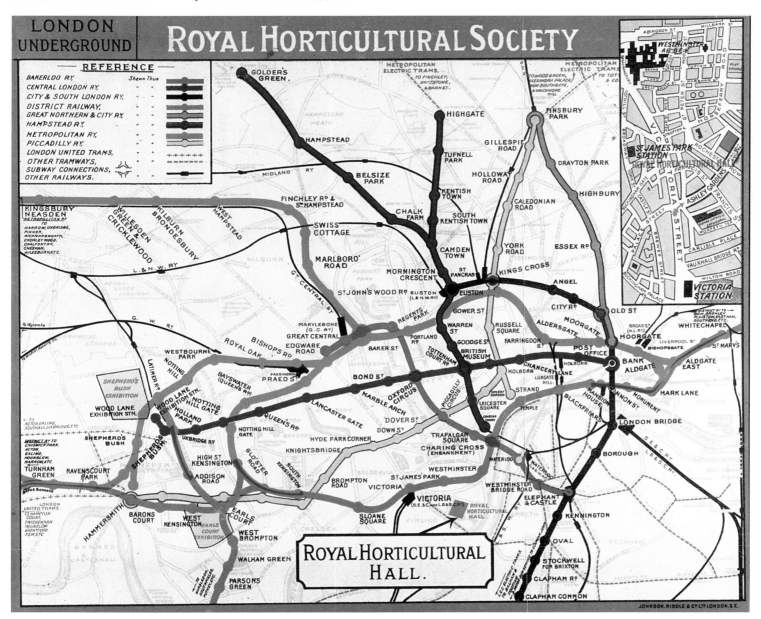

LONDON UNDERGROUND RAILWAYS 1909

9½ by 7¼ inches (24.5×18.5 cm)

The map and cover of this street plan booklet make prominent use of the new UNDERGROUND logo. Artwork for the coloured map and the blue overprints on the street plans were probably produced by Johnson Riddle & Co, the printers, while the street plans used the cartography of Kelly's Post Office directory. Because of the possibility of the colours of the Underground map (*top right*) being printed out of register, all lines have been given black outlines, with a consequent heavy effect. The street plans (*below*) show the prevailing geographic arrangement: *left*, the position of Hammersmith (Grove Road) and the Central London Railway loop at Wood Lane can be clearly seen; *centre*, the connection at Baker Street anticipates the 'corridor' joining interchanges favoured by Henry Beck on his diagrammatic maps; *right*, note the almost complete absence of buildings around Golders Green station!

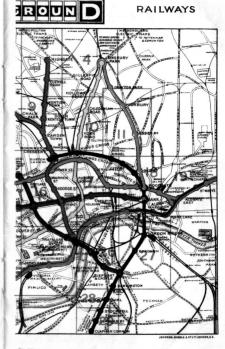

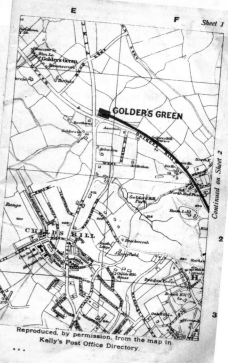

London Underground Railways
1909

10¾ by 8½ inches (27×22 cm)

This map was produced to go into a folder entitled 'The Excursionists' Guide with Map', which was aimed at leisure travellers, since the Underground was keen to entice them onto their relatively empty trains outside the rush hours.

The numbers on the map refer to points of interest which are listed on the cover side.

The clarity is instantly noticeable, especially by the elimination of all road details. Interestingly, the River Thames is retained even though it is not named. The depiction of the river may have followed experiments and discussions as to its future inclusion – discussions that were to be repeated regularly well into the diagrammatic map era.

While the yellow line has retained its black outline, the orange was seen to be dark enough to dispense with the use of highlighting. The two Euston stations have been separated, to avoid any doubt that trains may have run over each other's lines.

The fact that the Waterloo & City Railway was not given a colour, but just outlines, leads to the speculation that the Underground Group had given up any hope of swallowing it, since it was already safely in the hands of the wealthy London & South Western Railway. The inclusion of the two main line stations that could be used for travel to the Crystal Palace indicates that the Underground was aware that this was a very important leisure destination. LCC electric trams to Balham, Tooting and Clapham

Junction get a mention at Clapham Common, but there is no reference to the tram services northwards from Finsbury Park, Highgate and Golders Green.

53

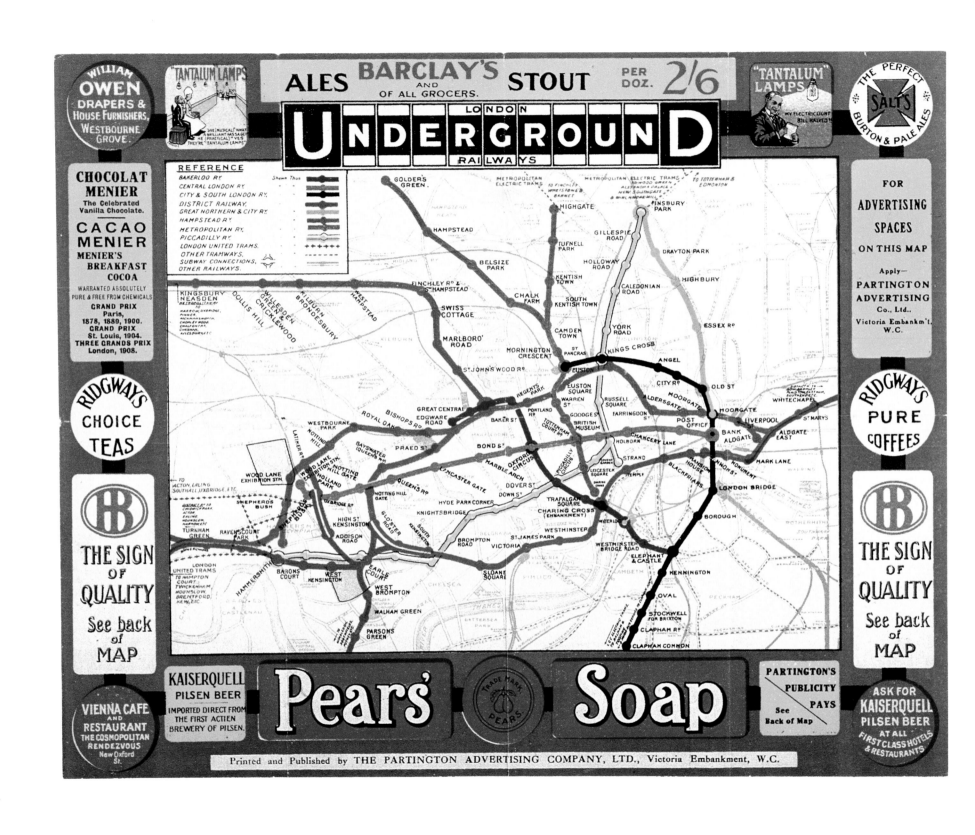

LONDON UNDERGROUND RAILWAYS 1909 (*left*)

10½ by 8½ inches (27×21.5 cm)

While the design of this map is drawn in the customary style of the period, it is the colourful and prominent nature of the many advertisements bordering the map that make it so distinctive. The Underground logo was still evolving, with the (experimental) inclusion of the words London and Railways within the white bars.

THE EVENING NEWS LONDON "TUBE MAP" c.1910 (*right*)

24¼ by 19¾ inches (62×50 cm)

The *Evening News* was one of many newspapers to sponsor maps, lending the perceived accuracy of their news coverage to that of the map. However, none actually produced the maps themselves – their own premises not being equipped for lithographic printing. This version was produced at the London Geographical Institute by George Philip & Son, using their own detailed maps as reference.

This map anticipates some of the

styles of conveying information adopted by the Underground for their own maps. While interchange stations use the Underground method of superimposing one line into the centre of the other, intermediate stations are shown as white circles outlined in black – a style used by George Philip on a production for the Underground in 1912.

The cover of this map deserves a special mention, for it is both charming and instructional. Whilst the depiction of the tube segments is not entirely correct (the segments are, in reality, bolted together from the inside) it does show graphically why the word *tube* was coined. The outer chain adds to the impression of great strength (an aspect that may have concerned visitors to London

considering using this novel method of transport). The number of segments equals the number of companies operating 'tube' railways, including the Waterloo & City (which did not belong to the Underground Group) and the Great Northern and City (which neither belonged to the Underground Group nor operated tube-sized trains). Nevertheless the GNCR did run

trains through tubes bored through London clay as opposed to digging trenches under streets and covering them over. The District, Metropolitan and East London, therefore, did not qualify for the cover, although their services are featured with equality on the actual map.

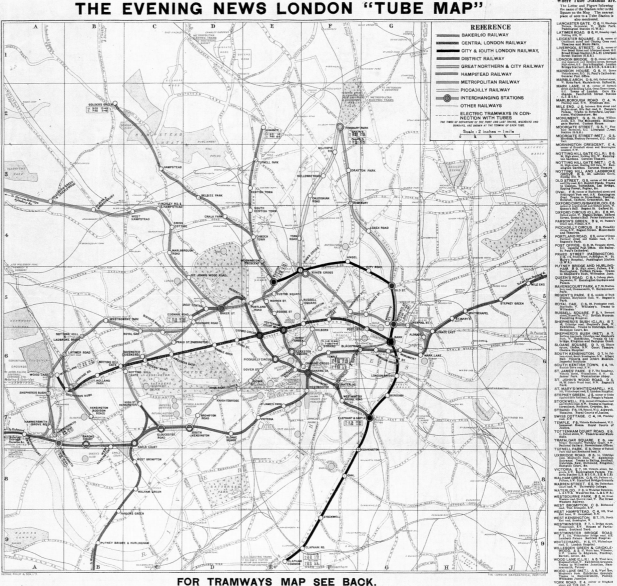

55

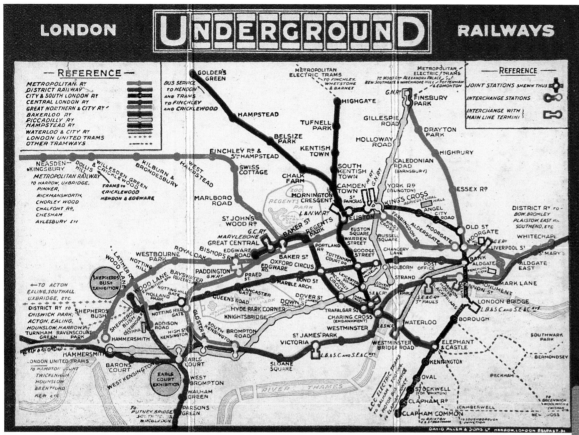

LONDON UNDERGROUND RAILWAYS c.1911

5¾ by 4¼ inches (15×11 cm)

This map, which opens up to three times its folded size, can be said to be the true ancestor of the modern tube map. The map, a development of the Excursionists' Guide (*shown on page 53*), has certain improvements and other additions, many of which were likely to be the result of meetings of interested parties representing all departments of the Underground Group.

The interchange circles are now shown in a more logical manner to differentiate between stations where changes could be made within one complex and those where the interchange stations were on different physical sites, but still close enough for a short walk. This interchange treatment has been extended to main line stations,

whether they be terminal or through stations. The City & South London has reverted to a dark colour similar to that of the Hampstead Tube.

Compared to the Excursionists' Guide, this map has had to be 'squeezed' to go into the reduced depth format. This can be seen mainly between Euston and Camden Town and in the area around Hammersmith, Earl's Court and Westbourne Park. Together with the increased information which has been included, this map appears busy to a degree that any information is difficult to find.

The cover is worth noting. The vertical Underground logo was frequently used as a sign outside stations, but less so on printed work. This handy sized pocket folder was the first to be printed on a linen backed thin card.

(*above*) Vertical sign, dating from before World War I, outside Gloucester Road station standing above an enamelled iron geographic Underground map of around 1932.

(*left*) The logo used vertically on the cover of the pocket map.

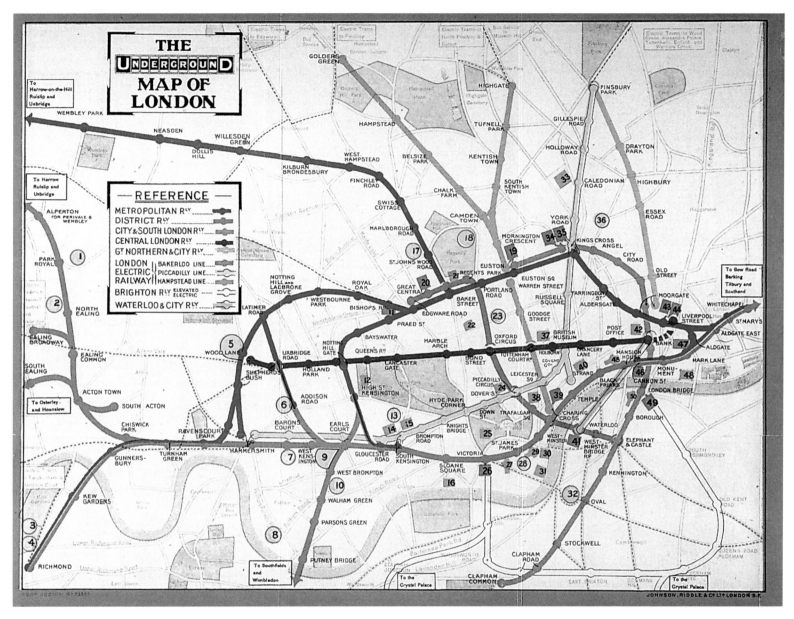

**THE UNDERGROUND MAP OF LONDON
1911**

10½ by 8 inches (27×20 cm)

The cartographers at Johnson Riddle & Co not only managed to produce a map more faithfully accurate to geography than had previously been achieved, but also managed to show more of the system in London's western suburbs. This meant that the Richmond terminus of the District and Metropolitan railways could be included.

At Hammersmith, all three stations are shown – of these, the District/Piccadilly and Hammersmith & City stations still survive, but the Metropolitan link between Ravenscourt Park and Shepherd's Bush, which was actually owned by the London & South Western Railway, was closed in June 1916, although part of the brick viaduct exists to this day and can be seen from the train to the east of Ravenscourt Park.

The London Brighton & South Coast Railway's lines serving Victoria and London Bridge, and those extending to Crystal Palace, were included on the map, following their electrification in 1909, although station names are only shown faintly.

To be able to include this line was helpful to the Underground Group since they had long recognised that the Crystal Palace was a good generator of off-peak travel.

This map was aimed primarily at the leisure traveller, with the inclusion of parks and, through the use of reference numbers on the map to a key on the cover side, places of interest and amusement, shopping centres, churches and chapels, picture galleries and theatres. Several exhibitions are featured on the cover, for which through tickets combining travel and admission price could be bought from all Underground stations.

LONDON UNDERGROUND RAILWAYS
1912

10½ by 8 inches (27×20 cm)

This forms an interesting comparison with the previous map (*on page 57*), for both were produced to the same size and only a year separated their issue. This version is on a slightly larger scale, but does not become any clearer for the change. The bold background of roads and main line railways swamps the Underground lines and their station names. Underground stations are indicated by black outlined white circles, which draw more attention to themselves than interchange stations receive. Paddington has reappeared as the main line station connecting its two

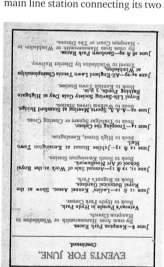

Underground stations (and its overlap onto the Bishop's Road station is accurate since the Metropolitan platforms form part of the suburban terminus of the GWR). Hammersmith, on the Metropolitan's line to Richmond has had 'Grove' added although the LSWR, owners of the station, referred to it in their timetables as Hammersmith Grove Road. Furthermore, photographs show that plain Hammersmith appeared on station signs.

The London Geographical Institute, which appears in the bottom right of the map, was the name used by George Philip & Son, an early cartographic firm which still exists today.

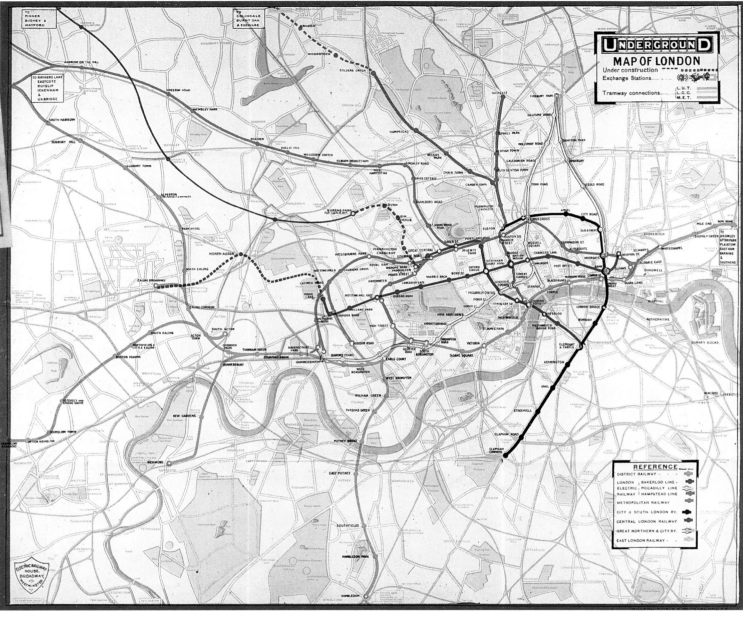

UNDERGROUND MAP OF LONDON 1913

14 by 11 inches (36×28 cm)

The incorporation of the Central London and City & South London railways into the Underground Group, along with the anticipated expansion of lines deeper into the suburbs, led to a substantial increase in the size of the map to cover a greater geographical area. This map, published in late 1913, takes in an area as far as Hounslow in the west and Wimbledon in the south.

Three projected extensions are also included: the Central London to Ealing Broadway; the Bakerloo to Queen's Park; and the Hampstead Tube to Edgware. These are all shown as being under construction. In anticipation of the Watford extension of the Bakerloo, the LNWR service between there and Queen's Park is also shown.

On the reverse side, on the title page, is included one of the first printed versions of the Underground bullseye, consisting of a solid red disc with the logo superimposed across it. This has been developed over nearly a century to form the blue and red roundel that exists today.

59

UNDERGROUND MAP OF LONDON
1914

16¾ by 13½ inches (42.5×34 cm)

The developments in clarity of the preceding maps demonstrated a continuing process while the system grew steadily larger and more intricate.

The cover side shows how the publication was again aimed at the leisure traveller, with some charming pictures of sights within central London. Small maps showing central London theatres and Underground connections to main

line stations are accompanied by a less usual map of the Chancery Lane area. The front cover sports the new bar and circle motif snugly within a latticed border, while the typography below is unexpectedly, but not unsuccessfully, ranged left.

The map, however, shows the result of an attempt to combine information from a number of maps onto one.

Economies

can be seen, in both style and the paper quality that was used, possibly due to World War I, although in 1914 the conflict was expected to be over by the end of that year. Experts in the craft of cartography and printing would have been drafted to war work, leaving unfamiliar hands in this technical field.

The resultant clutter means that the existing map as well as the new additional street plans have all lost the appeal of simplicity. The map itself has been reduced to one colour for Underground lines and red for the Metropolitan Railway. Also shown in bold form is the Great Central Railway, the last main line to reach London in March 1899. With its special printing of Marylebone Station at one end of the line and the Midlands and the North at the other end, it is possible that special maps were printed to cover the different routes to help unfamiliar travellers into London see easily the location of their London terminal station. The Central London Railway's extension from Shepherd's Bush was never to be built to Gunnersbury but went instead to its present terminus at Ealing Broadway.

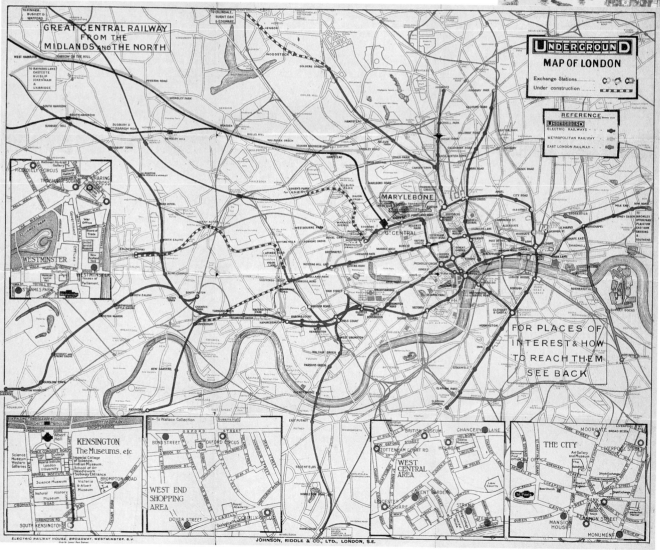

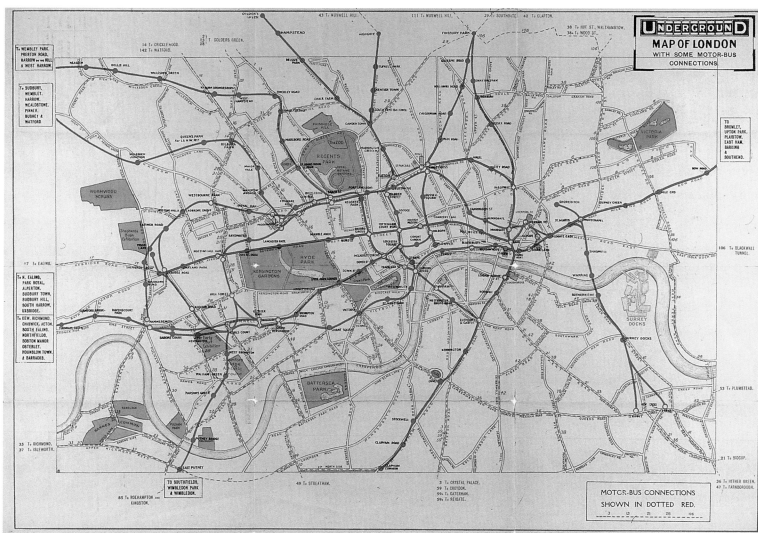

Underground Map of London
1916

18 by 11¾ inches (46×30 cm)

The Underground Group had taken over the London General Omnibus Company in 1912. With routes covering 1200 miles, the LGOC operated over an area six times larger than its parent company.

Motor buses were becoming more reliable (reliable enough for many to be sent to France during World War I as troop carriers) and were seen to be useful feeders to the comparatively expensive-to-run Underground.

The buses, with their drivers away on war duty, may provide a clue for producing this map, since the General would have been at pains to encourage transfer to the Underground. This map would have been produced with this interchange in mind, since no bus routes were shown over sections where Underground trains ran.

Although no printer is credited, it was probably drawn and printed by Johnson Riddle since the

Underground Map of London caption is in an identical style to those on other maps produced by them. On the reverse, the list of routes follows the format employed on contemporary bus maps.

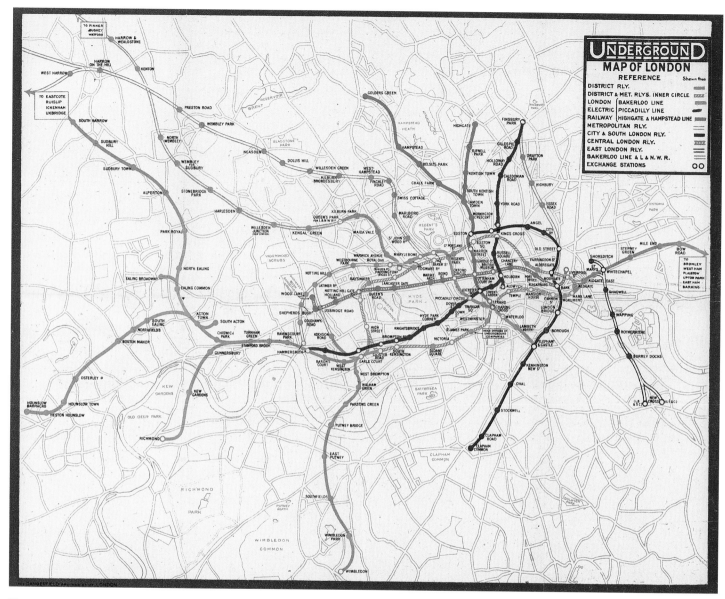

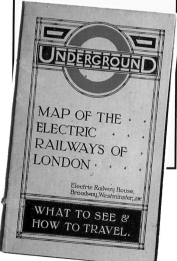

UNDERGROUND MAP OF LONDON 1919

14 by 11 inches (36×28 cm)

This map (the first since the Armistice of November 1918) marks a return to the colour coding of lines. While the colours are more limited than hitherto, some are now in hues that are very familiar.

For the first time the Piccadilly appears in blue, while the Hampstead Tube (described in the key as the Hampstead & Highgate Line) appears in solid red. The Bakerloo and District have kept their brown and green respectively, while the Metropolitan – including the Great Northern & City which had been taken over by the Metropolitan in 1913 – is shown in outline green. For the first time the Inner Circle has been given a separate treatment of hatched green.

Apart from the East London Line, all lines over which full size trains ran are indicated by various treatments of green. With the London & North Western line to Watford also shown as outline, a certain logic now existed in that all non-Underground Group lines were shown in a consistent style.

The Metropolitan no longer extends to Richmond, the connecting line with its station at Hammersmith Grove Road having closed for good in 1916. The faint unnamed street plan (only parks are named), devoid of main line railways, forms an unobtrusive background.

A considerable development to map presentation was the update of the Underground Group's distinctive logo, using the new typeface commissioned by the Underground and designed by the calligrapher Edward Johnston. This is shown on the map side, and also on the cover in conjunction with the newly proportioned red circle with white 'eye'. However, this 'bullseye' has merely replaced the older style, giving the cover, with the type unaltered below, a slightly uneasy look.

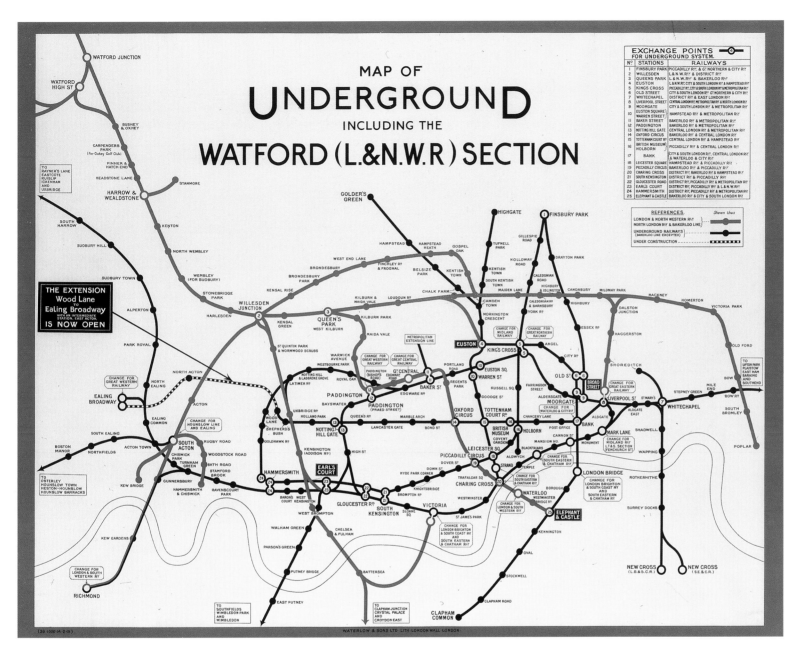

WATERLOW & SONS LTD LITH LONDON WALL LONDON.

MAP OF THE UNDERGROUND INCLUDING THE WATFORD (L&NWR) SECTION 1919

50 by 40 inches (127×102 cm)

This would more correctly be entitled Map of the London & North Western suburban and the Bakerloo lines including the Underground. The entire LNWR lines (including its services over the West London Extension Railway to Clapham Junction and beyond) are shown prominently in red, while the Underground lines are in thinner dark blue lines.

The Metropolitan Railway extension is shown merely as a stub from Baker Street, which is understandable since this line would provide competitive services for much of the way out to Watford.

Because the Underground is reduced to one colour, lines at interchange stations are referenced by number to the key where the connecting lines are spelt out. The extension of the Central London Railway to Ealing Broadway has an overprinted panel announcing it as being open, which did not, in fact, take place until August of the following year.

Lettering is a copy of Edward Johnston's type that had recently come into use on the Underground of which Waterlows, who printed this map, would have held the fonts for use on letterpress posters. The logo in this style, with the tops of all the letters aligning, was never actually used by the Underground, which leads to the conclusion the LNWR played a leading role in the development of this map.

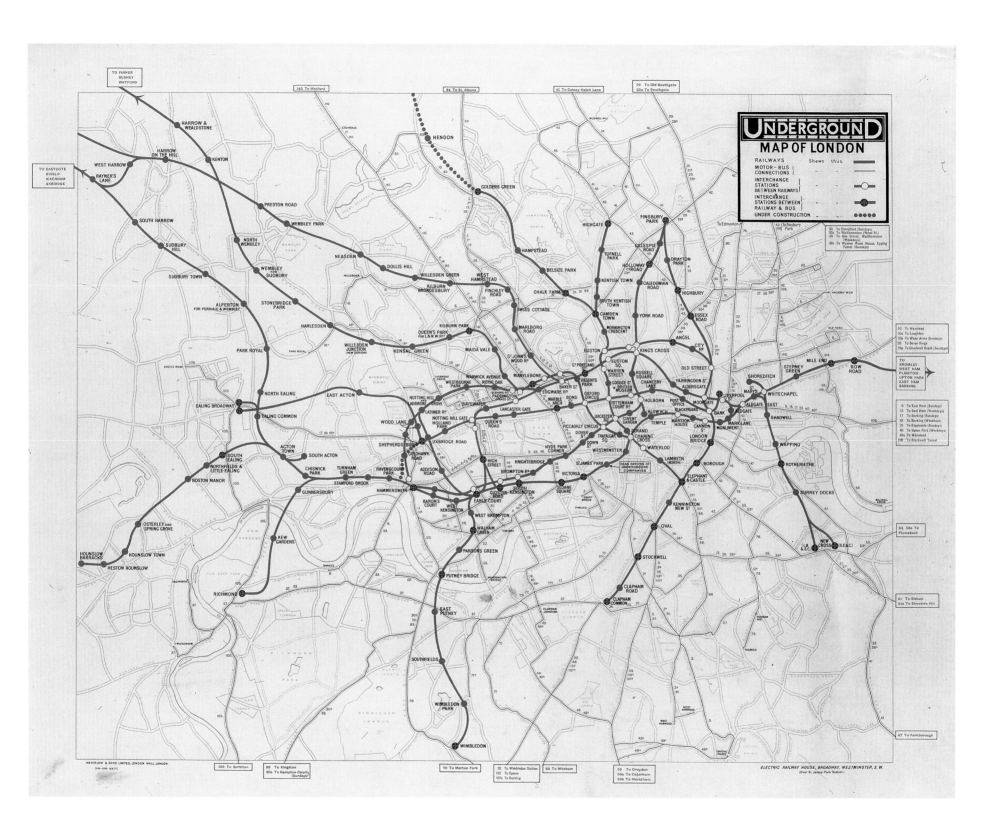

64

UNDERGROUND MAP OF LONDON

1921 *(left)*

50 *by* 40 *inches* (127×102 cm)

This map shows the Underground network (including Metropolitan Railway routes), as well as what are described as 'motor bus connections' – presumably the General and its associates. The interesting extension shown as being under construction is that of the Central London Railway between Shepherd's Bush and Ravenscourt Park over the connection built by the LSWR.

UNDERGROUND MAP OF ELECTRIC RAILWAYS OF LONDON 1921

14 *by* 11 *inches* (36×28 cm)

This map, like the one on page 62, was printed by the Dangerfield Printing Company. But, by using calligraphy instead of the more usual block lettering, together with the decorative borders, a very attractive effect has been achieved.

On this map the background, including the river, has been removed altogether. The style and area of the lines remain, apart from some cropping at the top because of the altered proportion of the paper. Interchange stations retain white centres to the circles and Camden Town has been added. The Metropolitan Railway once again uses maroon as its line colour, the Inner Circle loses its separate identity and the East London Railway becomes green, thereby appearing to be a branch of the District Railway. Eastbound District Railway services are indicated as terminating at Southend, acknowledging the service run between there and Ealing Broadway, jointly with the London Tilbury & Southend Railway using their rolling stock and District Railway electric locomotives over the Underground section. The information within boxes has been increased to include details previously included on the cover side.

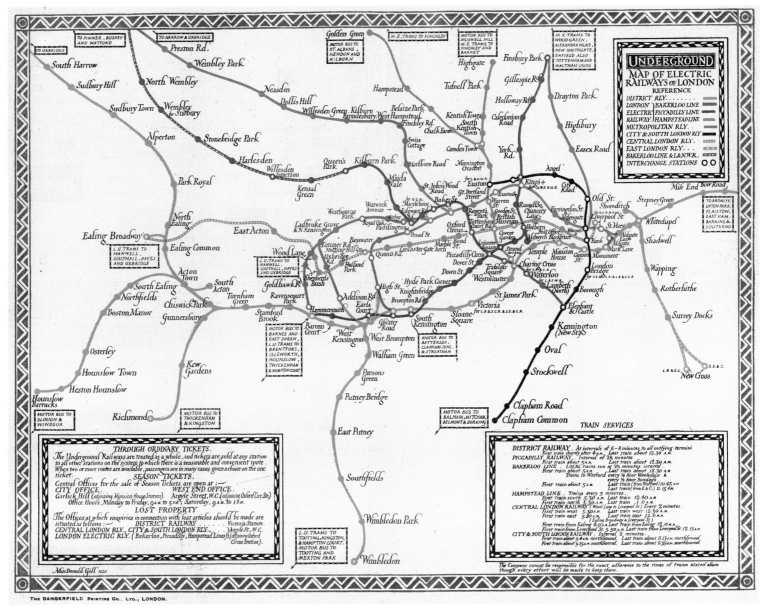

65

Chapter 5

The decade of designers

Until the 1920s the charm that we now admire in the early maps could be said to be coincidental. We have seen the gradual development of the traditional map as produced by cartographic companies, and from them to those maps produced in printers' studios as an experimental art form. The artists within printers' studios were expert copiers – as they, and their colleagues in commercial art studios, have continued to be until recent times. But it was in the 1920s that a generation of creative artists and designers were brought in to add their skills to solving the problem of communicating the Underground network in the simplest and most understandable way possible.

Frank Pick had already commissioned the calligrapher, Edward Johnston, to design a letterform to be used on signs and posters. Another calligrapher, MacDonald (Max) Gill, was brought in to have a look at the Underground map. Max was born in 1884, two years after his more famous brother, Eric. Both received lessons in calligraphy from Edward Johnston, combining this skill with letter cutting on stone and (in the case of Max) the painting of murals. This small art movement of the Johnstons and the Gills, based in a Sussex village, was to be bound even closer when Max developed a relationship with Edward Johnston's daughter.

MacDonald Gill's work spawned a number of artistically based maps. Designed and drawn in the best traditions of penmanship, they were aimed more at the casual visitor rather than the serious traveller using the Underground as a means of getting about as part of earning a living. But they lacked the urgency of travelling quickly between stations, being ready to leave trains to change onto others and to "mind the doors", "pass down the car"

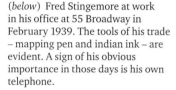

(below) Fred Stingemore at work in his office at 55 Broadway in February 1939. The tools of his trade – mapping pen and indian ink – are evident. A sign of his obvious importance in those days is his own telephone.

(right) Tailpiece drawn by Stingemore for the Railway Magazine and used for about a ten year period until World War II.

and "let 'em off first"! Most also relied on a background of streets, parks and the River Thames to set the tube lines in context.

The Underground Group's in house artist provided a contrasting solution.

F H Stingemore (1891-1954)

Fred Stingemore entered the Publicity Manager's office of the Underground Group around 1919 from the Temple Press as (what was described at the time as) a draughtsman. Drawing maps and plans to illustrate Underground publications, he was later appointed personal draughtsman to the Underground Group's general manager, Frank Pick. He took on the drawing of the pocket railway map from 1924.

The Commercial Drawing Office, which survived until the 1980s, was the source of the vast volume of technical drawings, maps, plans and calligraphic lettering decorating retirement certificates, long service awards and official invitations that this large organisation generated. Stingemore headed this department until his death in office in 1954.

His spare time activities included the taking of over 10,000 photographs – between 1909 and 1939 his glass negatived camera recorded rural and railway subjects in the West Country, north Yorkshire, the Lake District and his native Hertfordshire. His pictures of moving trains required considerable skill with slower exposure films if blurring was to be avoided.

In addition to designing a number of posters for Underground Group companies, through the 1920s and early '30s he produced a series of illustrations for article heads and tails in the Railway Magazine, as well as for the Underground's own *TOT Magazine*.

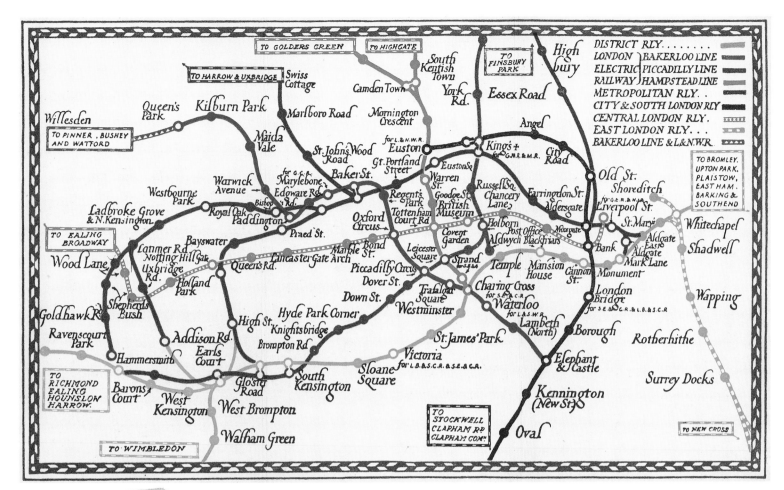

**INNER AREA [UNDERGROUND] MAP OF
ELECTRIC RAILWAYS OF LONDON 1921**

8 by 4¾ inches (20×12.5 cm)

This map was one of the first
examples of a style which combined
the talents of artist and technician. It
is the work of MacDonald Gill who,
while building on former designs,
has added his own personalised style
of calligraphy for the station names
and text in the key boxes.

As a companion to the map shown
on page 65, this card folder, which
was printed on linen-backed card for
durability, covered central London
only. But even at this scale certain
areas are becoming congested,
notably around the City where a
large number of stations are
concentrated within a compact
space.

(*right*) MacDonald Gill supervising
his assistant in his studio in 1930.
His work also included murals in the
dining saloons of the great Cunard
White Star liners, *Queen Mary* and
Queen Elizabeth.

67

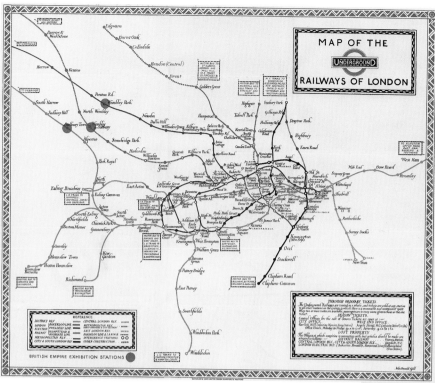

MAP OF THE UNDERGROUND RAILWAYS OF LONDON 1923 (*this page*)
18 by 14½ inches (45.5×37 cm)

Using similar artwork to the preceding maps, this was printed by Waterlows who were probably printing the quad royal poster maps already, the proportions of both being the same. The seeds of the resumption of building work, following the end of World War I, are shown on the map with the extensions to Edgware and Morden, and the link from Charing Cross to join with the City & South London at Kennington, which were all to open by 1926.

Two border designs are used, both having been used separately on the 1921 maps. On the map side, the one concession to the Underground's house lettering is where Edward Johnston's Underground type forms the title, adding weight to the assumption that this pocket map was a photographic reduction from the poster. The cover (*right*), using Johnston's sans serif type,

harmonises with those being produced by the London General Omnibus Company, as does the size of the map when folded.

MAP OF THE UNDERGROUND RAILWAYS OF LONDON 1924 (*right*)
18 by 14½ inches (45.5×37 cm)

With a focus on central London, this map also attempts to show the hinterland covered by the Underground system. By deploying a coloured background to depict this area, it has been possible to leave the streets in white, instead of drawing them in outline. Emphasis has been given to the railway lines by edging them either side in white. The line colours have again changed – the Central London is now hatched green and the Bakerloo is red. The most significant changes are, however, to the Hampstead Tube and the City & South London

Railway, which have been combined as black and given the overall title of the Hampstead & Highgate Line.

While the station names on the map have reverted to block lettering, the text forming the title and references utilises a typeface with calligraphic qualities.

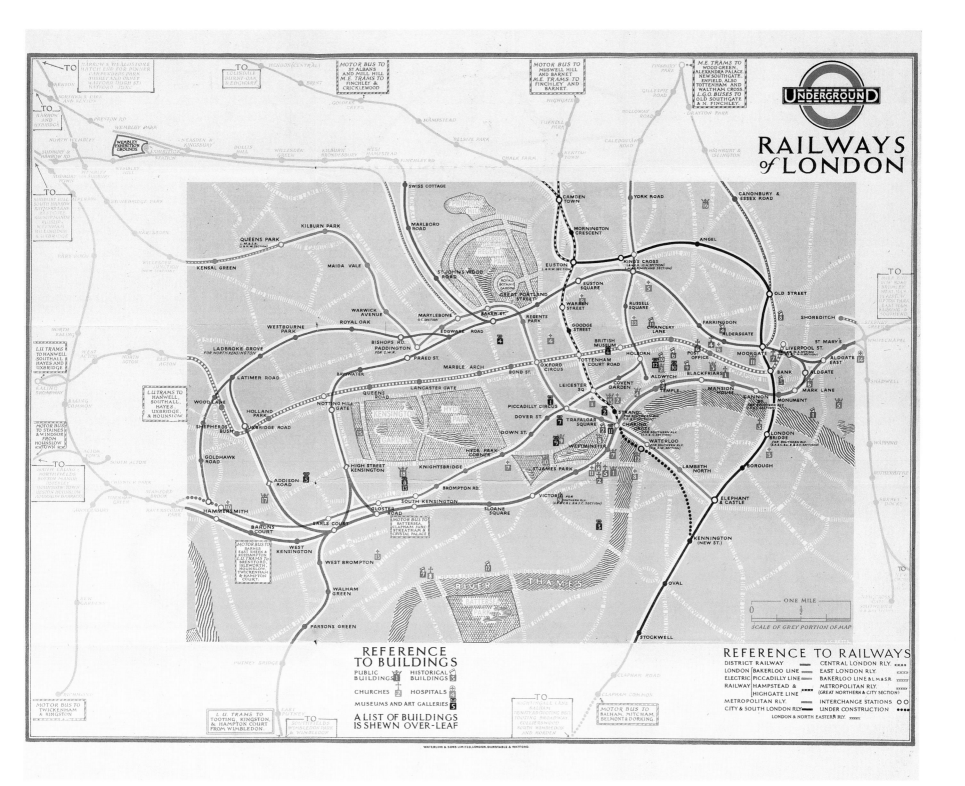

RAILWAYS of LONDON

UNDERGROUND

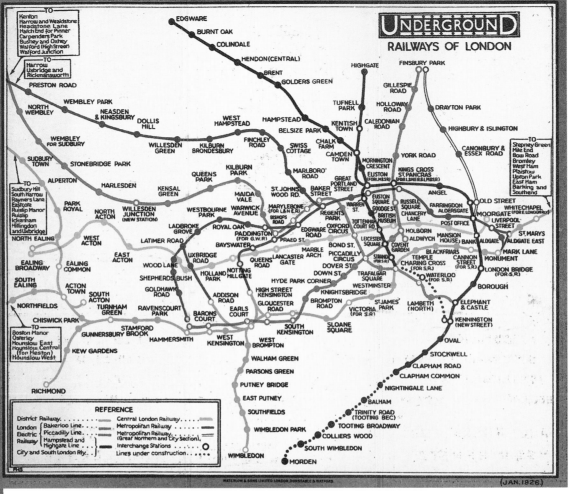

UNDERGROUND RAILWAYS OF LONDON 1926

6 by 5 inches (15×13 cm)

This is one of a series of pocket maps which remained in a similar format from 1925 until replaced by Henry Beck's diagrammatic version in 1933.

Designed by Fred Stingemore, it combines the best and clearest features of the maps from the preceding two decades. Although using geographic representation, some lines have been 'twisted' to fit into the area.

Stations are indicated by solid circles, while interchange stations between Underground lines are shown as open circles, as are others which connect with the main line railways. Interchange stations which are distinctly separated are shown with open circles for each line, while those interchanges where all the platforms are within the same complex share a circle.

This ruling is broken at Earl's Court and Hammersmith on the District and Piccadilly. Bayswater and Lancaster Gate are shown as interchanges while Queens Road is not. British Museum, on the Central London Railway, is shown as an interchange with the Piccadilly Line at Holborn, although the latter's name looks as if it could refer to what is in fact Chancery Lane. Aldwych is shown as an interchange, presumably with Temple.

Some line colours have again changed, for example the Central London has become orange. The East London Railway has disappeared altogether (for it had been transferred to the Southern Railway), although Whitechapel is shown as an interchange.

Meanwhile, after about 20 years of being condensed to Gloster Rd, Gloucester Road is, at last, spelt out in full.

The Stingemore maps were, in their way, as distinctive as those developed later by Beck. Their brightly coloured linen backed covers, small size and absence of topographical detail made them instantly recognisable – the first series of true pocket maps.

The use of sans serif type may have diminished the decorative splendour of MacDonald Gill's designs, but made the necessarily small text more readable and the maps themselves more functional.

On this example from January 1926, the City & South London Railway's extension to Morden and its link with the Hampstead & Highgate Line between Charing Cross and Kennington are still shown as being under construction, although both were to open in September of the same year. For the first time, these still separate railways are shown in black, symbolising their close connection which culminated in the renaming of both as the Northern Line in the late 1930s, when even more extensions were being planned and built.

UNDERGROUND RAILWAYS OF LONDON 1931

6½ by 5½ inches (17×14.5 cm)

Between 1925 and 1933, the Stingemore design was produced in 13 separate editions on card folders, and some were printed on paper for insertion into guidebooks. In 1927 the size was increased by three quarters of an inch (19 mm), allowing the map size to be enlarged, instead of the alternative option of expanding the area of London covered.

The River Thames was included and station names printed in their respective line colours. Both these amendments were probably made following suggestions from interested departmental heads. Interchange stations had to compromise with one or other of their line colours. Some station names cut across lines when they need not have. For example, Wood Lane and Shepherd's Bush names referring to the Central London Railway stations could have been moved so as not to break into the Metropolitan Railway's line. Notting Hill Gate could perhaps have been repositioned so as not to break into the purple line. A number of little arrows have been drawn against station names, implying that better solutions could not be found to position names closer to their stations.

While these comments might be considered to be rather unsympathetic, it should be acknowledged (in these days of computers) that the artwork for this map would have been drawn with

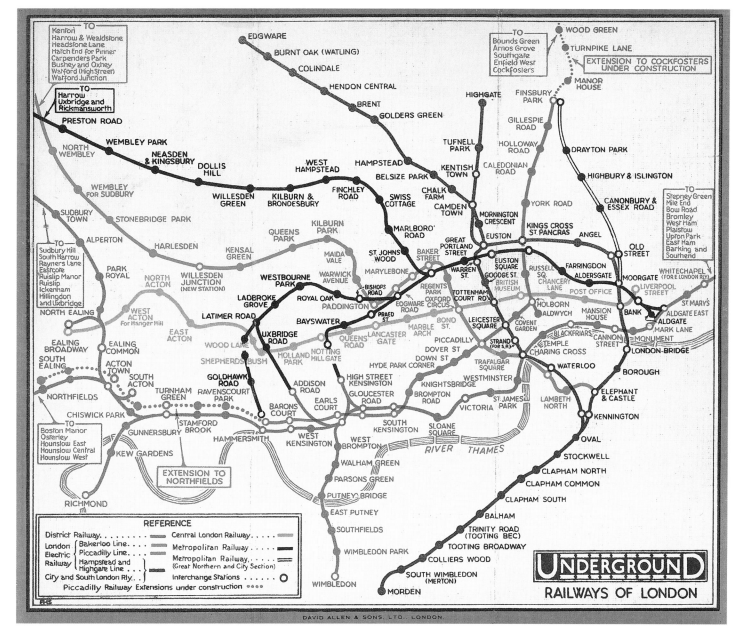

mapping pen and ink and used again, with modifications, for each issue. Changes to the artwork would be made by scratching out the area to be deleted with a razor blade, and redrawing the amendment onto a surface that had then lost much of its smoothness.

The two extensions on the Piccadilly Line are shown as being under construction.

The route to Hounslow made use, as far as Turnham Green, of the redundant tracks over which the Metropolitan Railway's trains had run to Richmond until during World War I. The rest of the route to Hounslow was to share the line with

the District, which may explain why the note in the box omits 'under construction', since it was more accurately a conversion.

The eastern route is shown as extending to Lordship Lane, although this station was to open in September 1932 as Wood Green.

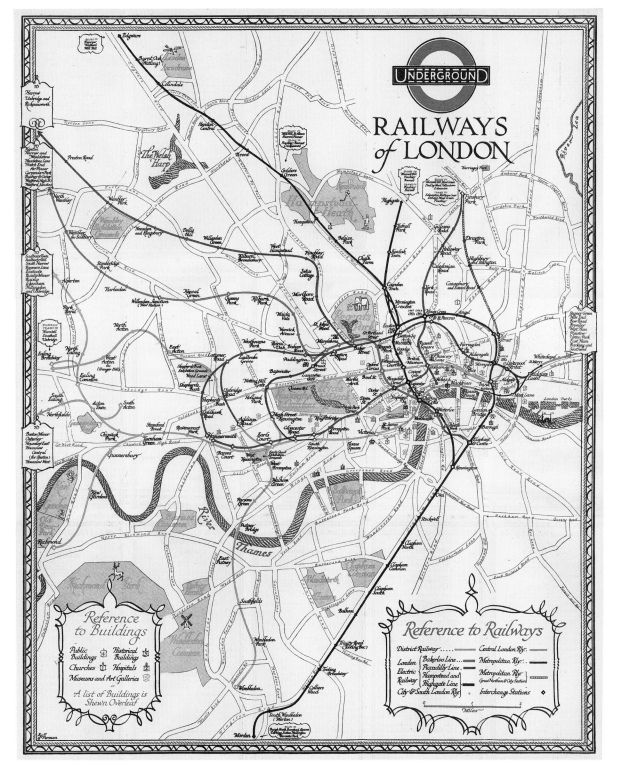

UNDERGROUND RAILWAYS OF LONDON 1928 (*left*)

14½ by 17½ inches (37×45 cm)

Whilst the Stingemore folders were functional in both size and information, this map is aimed at the visitor to London, as may be judged from the extensive travel and tourist information on the cover side.

This very decorative map was designed by E G Perman utilising hand-drawn calligraphy throughout. The geography is accurate to the extent that a kink in the River Lea qualifies it for inclusion within the rectangular border.

The style of the lines, stations and interchanges follows very closely that used on the Stingemore map.

The cover side gives a host of information, including a special map showing main line terminal station connections, which indicates that this map was destined for people living beyond the limits of the Underground system. The place for this folder was at home with the telephone book and local bus and train timetables. The functionality of the Underground bullseye shows how happily it can co-exist with a traditionally Roman typeface.

UNDERGROUND MAP OF LONDON 1930 (*right*)

50 by 40 inches (127×102 cm)

The Underground lines have been drawn in the same style as on Stingemore's pocket maps, but since they are superimposed on a geographical road and rail map of London and its suburbs, they follow true geography faithfully.

This map was a precursor of what, after World War II, became known as the London's Transport Systems map, which continued production until the mid-1970s.

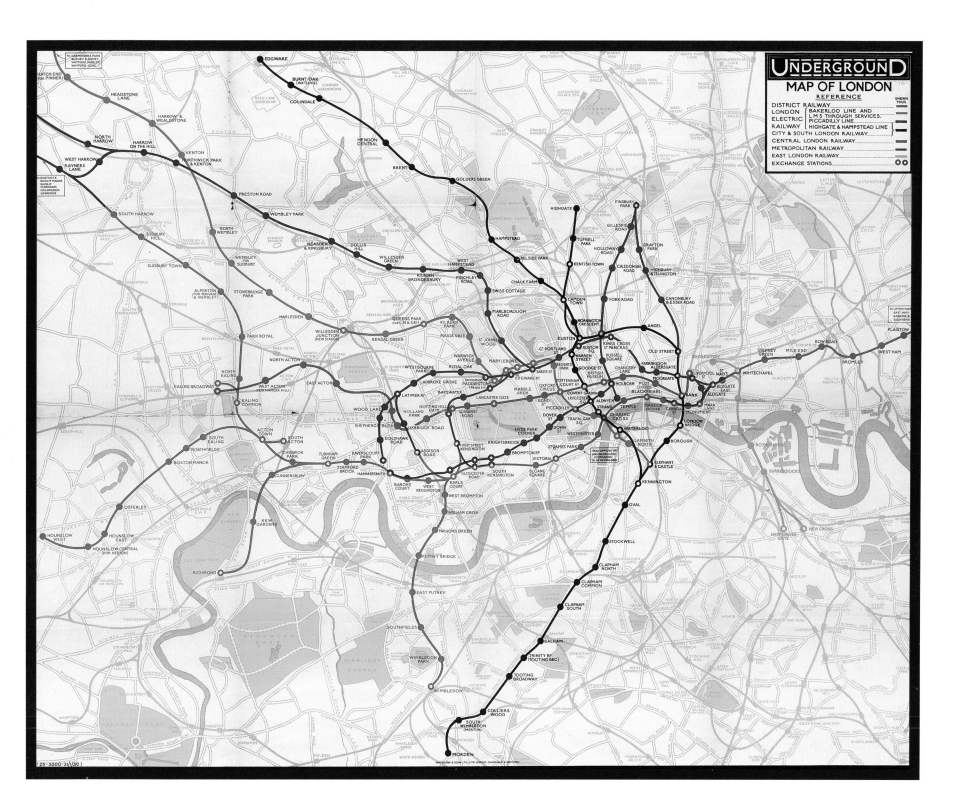

UNDERGROUND MAP OF CENTRAL LONDON 1932

13¼ by 10¾ inches (33.5×27 cm)

The Underground continued to explore ways in which London's streets, shops, parks and theatres could be made clearer to locate for visitors. Consequently, there was sometimes a need to show the tube lines superimposed onto a street plan. This version traces the lines very delicately in such a way that they do not swamp the important street names. Main line railways have been included (but not the Waterloo & City Railway) in their entirety, where the locations of their termini would probably have sufficed. Extensions at both ends of the Piccadilly Line are shown in map insets, for the Underground seized every opportunity to attract local traffic into central London. The border is worth noting, since it was this item which received constant attention, not only by the Underground companies but also by the main line railways, in order to appear as friendly and personal organisations.

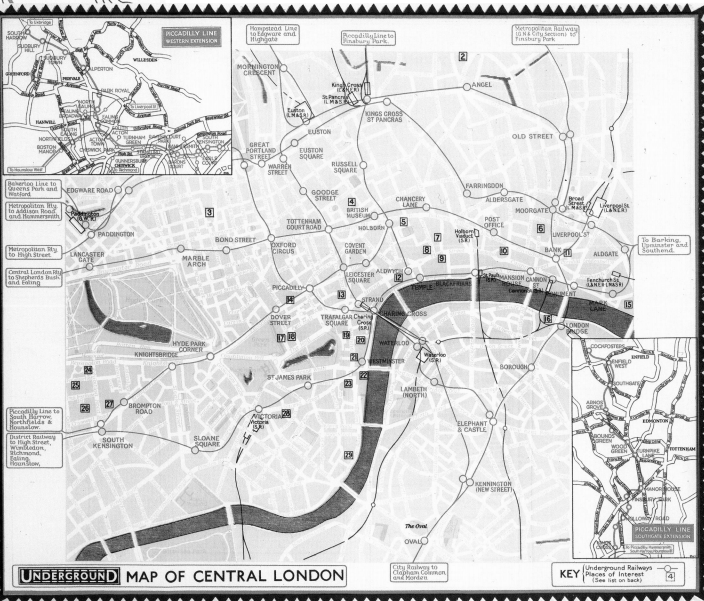

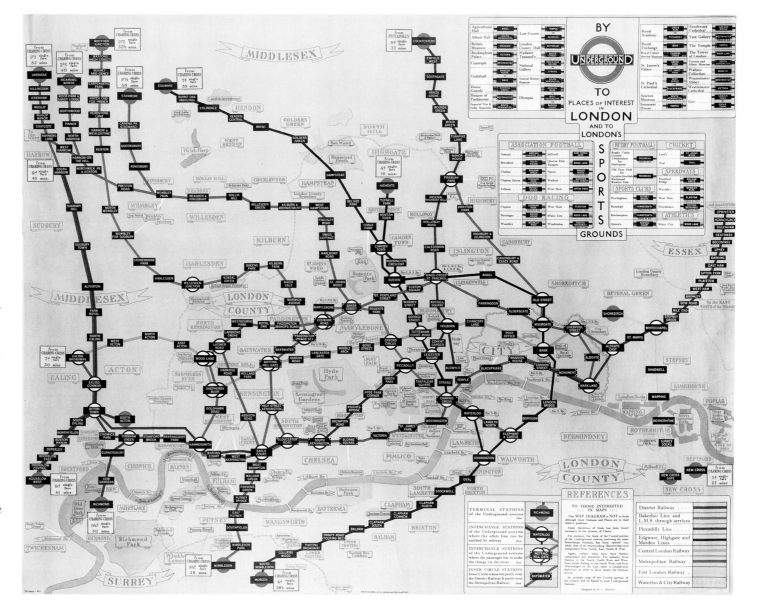

BY UNDERGROUND TO PLACES OF INTEREST IN LONDON AND TO LONDON'S SPORTS GROUNDS 1933

50 by 40 inches (127×102 cm)

This charming and colourful map could be described as schematic (although the designer called it a diagram), in that the railway routes roughly follow their geographical alignments but corners have been reduced to a minimum and in nearly all cases are hidden under station names.

Geography has been distorted to get the entire Underground system within the area of the poster, which has made the north west suburbs appear to be very well served. Indeed, the designer, A L Gwynne, has been considerate enough to explain in Victorian phraseology the motives for the arriving at the appearance of this map, under the heading of **References:**

*The **Map Diagram** is **not** to scale although most Stations and Places are in their relative positions.*
Some distortion of Scale has been found necessary in the interest of Clarity.

For instance, the Scale of the Central portion of the Underground System, enclosing the main Interchange Stations, has been opened out, while that of the Surrounding Districts has been compressed from North, East, South & West.

Again, certain lines have been further compressed and distorted. For instance, from Harrow to the North, North West, and West, from South Ealing to the South West, and from Whitechapel to the East, there is considerable distortion in order to show clearly the Stations served.

An accurate map of the Central portion of the System will be found in most Underground Stations.

Journey times and fares from Charing Cross are given and since they are based on distance, they do give an indication of the length of journeys that the map does not.

The stark representation of the Underground lines and stations contrasts with the traditional treatment of the background, with its names within scrolls.

The Docks around Poplar seem a bit over-detailed since they were so far from any Underground lines.

As will be seen from the key, terminal stations are given solid red discs behind their names (except Upminster, where there is a note about services to Southend, and Ealing Broadway, which is treated as an interchange station.

Inner Circle stations have the corners of their nameboards nicked.

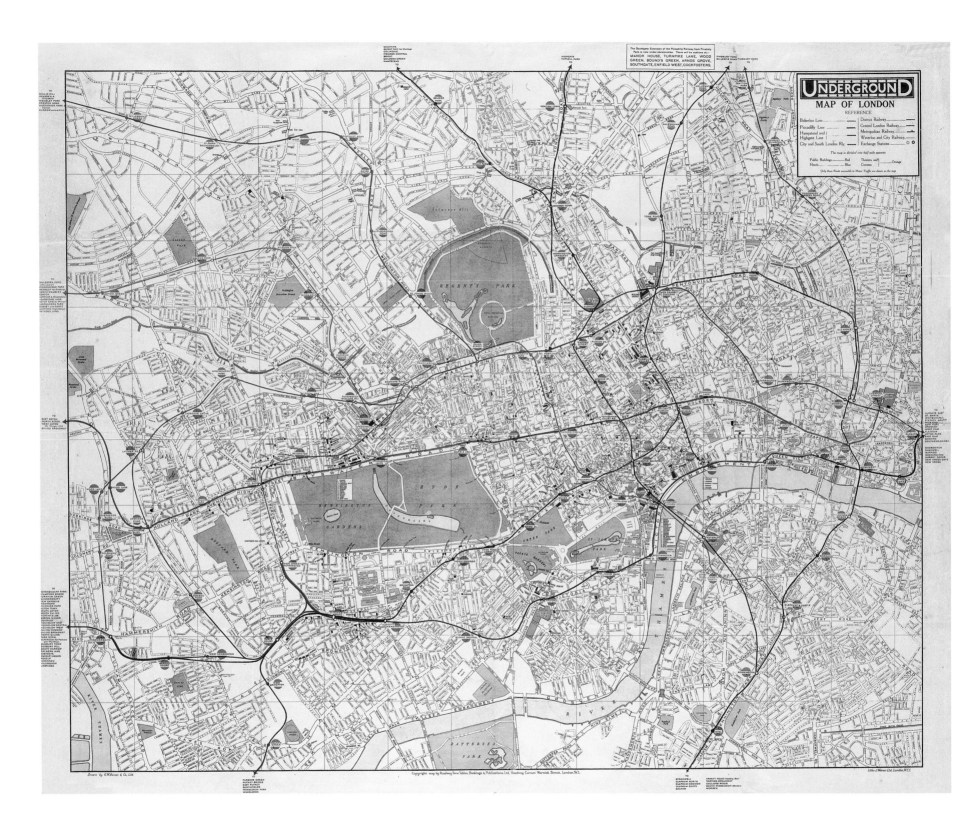

UNDERGROUND MAP OF LONDON

1932 (*entire map left, details this page*)
50 by 40 inches (127×102 cm)

Underground routes from the suburbs, with their stations forming local focal points, to central London were shown adequately on different maps, whether by geographical means or in diagrammatic form (already well established as a means of showing lines in car interiors). However, it was more difficult to show locations of stations within the central area without the assistance of a street plan. This poster example

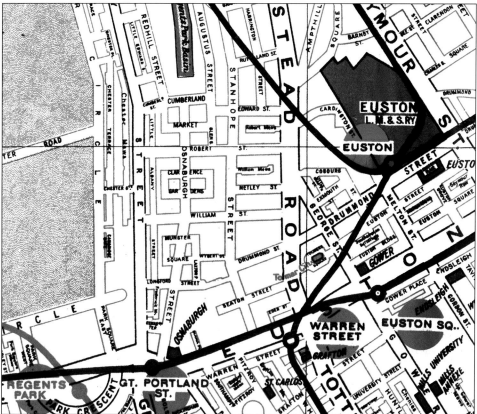

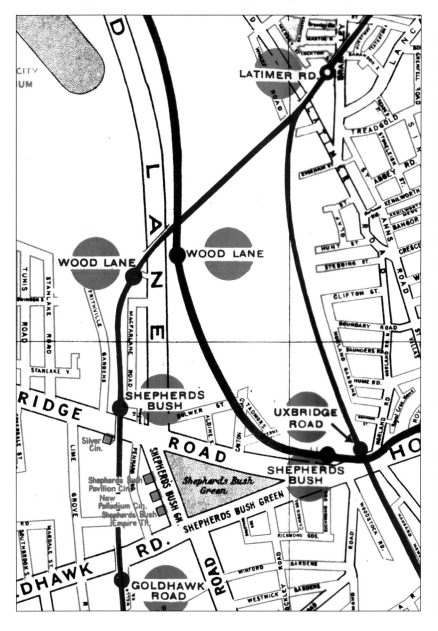

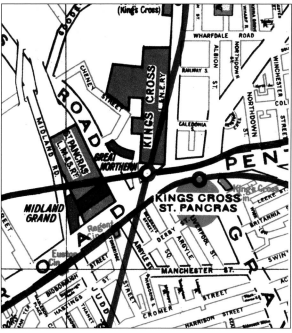

is very detailed and is probably equalled only by the A-Z map series in booklet form. The lines are shown finely so as not to disturb the process of searching for a particular street.

The red discs denoting stations are to a style which had been replaced about 15 years earlier by the bar and circle bullseye, although plenty existed on station platforms. However, they are still very effective (showing the success of the bullseye, even in a minute form). Small lettering in the margins gives an indication of the area from which lines originate. These are illustrated here half the size they appear on the poster.

This map, drawn by the cartographic firm of G W Bacon (publishers of, amongst others, large scale street plans of London), was printed lithographically by J Weiner Ltd.

UNDERGROUND MAP OF LONDON 1933

Various sizes to suit local conditions

As well as being printed on paper for pasting on panels, mounting in frames or on card and cloth, maps of the Underground system were also manufactured, from around 1910, as large vitreous enamelled steel panels for display outside or near stations. Primarily used as an aid to route finding, they were also regarded as an important means of promoting the service.

This massive 4-panel map, installed at Kilburn in the early 1930s, was produced in vitreous enamel by Chromo of Wolverhampton, who also manufactured many enamel panel advertisements for well known companies. Enamelled maps (and, of course, signs) were favoured over paper for outdoor locations because of their robustness and longevity. However, it was for these reasons that, with the constant expansion of the Underground system, they were rendered obsolete almost as soon as they were erected. This map includes the extensions to Cockfosters, South Harrow and Hounslow West of the Piccadilly Line, which had all opened by October 1933. However, the Stanmore branch of the Metropolitan Railway is omitted, even though services had commenced a year earlier. This map was also produced in paper versions, some mounted on fabric for wall hanging, to various sizes.

A smaller and less extensive version of this map was discovered at Temple station during renovations. It can still be seen to the right of the station entrance, where it has been preserved within a blue panel.

STATIONS RENAMED

NAME ON MAP	NOW KNOWN AS
GREAT CENTRAL	MARYLEBONE
WESTMINSTER BRIDGE ROAD	LAMBETH (NORTH)
STRAND	ALDWYCH
CHARING CROSS (HAMPSTEAD LINE)	STRAND FOR S. E. & C. RLY.
PORTLAND ROAD	GT. PORTLAND STREET

A NEW STATION KENSAL GREEN HAS BEEN OPENED BETWEEN QUEENS PARK AND WILLESDEN (BAKERLOO LINE) ALSO THE EXTENSION EALING BROADWAY TO WOOD LANE.

Copies of this Map size 13½" × 11" may be obtained upon application to any member of the staff.

PAPER STICKER

Although vitreous enamel maps were popular as an alternative to the constant reposting of paper maps, it was their very longevity which brought about their demise. Until new maps were fixed, adhesive stickers were printed for the old maps, advising of any changes to the system. This sticker is from 1921.

By Underground 1932

6 by 6 inches (15.5×15.5 cm)

The Underground could also produce maps in a semi-decorative form to promote travel as in this example for school children. Designed by Freda Lingstrom, it has been hand lettered entirely by her. The cover side is, if anything, even more attractive.

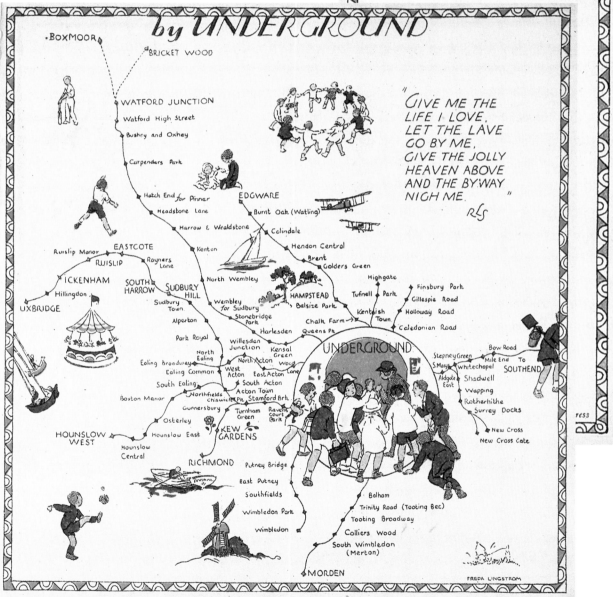

Bibliography

Anon, **Art For All:** *London Transport Posters 1908–1947*, Art and Technics, 1949.

Baglee, Christopher and Morley, Andrew, **Street Jewellery:**
a history of enamel advertising signs, New Cavendish, 1978.

Bancroft, Peter, **London Transport Records at the Public Record Office (part one)**,
Nebulous Books, 1996.

Barker, T C and Robbins, Michael, **A History of London Transport**,
Vols 1 and 2, Allen & Unwin, London, 1963, 1974.

Barman, Christian, **The Man who Built London Transport:** *a biography of Frank Pick*,
David & Charles, Newton Abbot, 1979.

Bruce, J Graeme and Croome, Desmond F, **The Twopenny Tube**, Capital Transport, 1996.

Croome, Desmond F., **The Piccadilly Line**, Capital Transport, 1998.

Garland, Ken, **Mr Beck's Underground Map**, Capital Transport, 1994.

Green, Oliver, **Underground Art**, Studio Vista, London, 1990.

Horne, Mike and Bayman, Bob, **The Northern Line**, Capital Transport, 1999.

Hyde, Ralph, **Printed Maps of Victorian London: 1851–1900**, Wm Dawson, 1975.

MacCarthy, Fiona, **Eric Gill**, Faber & Faber, 1989.

Smith, G Royde, **The History of Bradshaw**, Henry Blacklock & Company, Manchester, 1939.

Rose, Douglas, **The London Underground: a diagrammatic history**, Douglas Rose, 1999.

Wakeman, Geoffrey and Bridsen, Gavin, **A Guide to Nineteenth Century Colour Printers**,
The Plough Press, Loughborough, 1975.